RELIGIOUS ETHICS IN AFRICA

Peter Kasenene

Fountain Publishers

Fountain Publishers Ltd.
P.O. Box 488
Kampala, Uganda

© Peter Kasenene 1998
First Published 1998

All rights reserved. No part of this publication may be reproduced, stored in a retrieval system or transmitted in any form or by any means electronic, mechanical, photocopying, recording or otherwise without the prior written permission of the publisher.

ISBN 9970 02 133 8

CONTENTS

Preface ii

Acknowledgements iv

Chapter One: **Introduction** 1

Chapter Two: **Ethical Theory** 8

Chapter Three: **Religion, Ethics and Morality** 17

Chapter Four: **Preservation and Promotion of One's Life** 25

Chapter Five: **Respect for Other People's Lives** 39

Chapter Six: **Sex Outside Marriage** 56

Chapter Seven: **Marriage** 71

Chapter Eight: **Family Life** 87

Chapter Nine: **Conclusion** 101

References 106

ACKNOWLEDGEMENT

I am deeply grateful to my students at the University of Swaziland and the Institute of Teacher Education, Kyambogo, for their contribution through both formal and informal discussions and for their resourceful comments and responses to the lecture notes which formed the basis of this book.

Besides the works cited and those indicated in the bibliography, I drew invaluable information from the lecture notes on ethics by Fr. O. Macgrath. I am very grateful to him for making them available to me. I am also grateful to Mr. M. Dlamini, the Director of the Islamic Information Services in Swaziland, Fr. R. McDonnel, a Chaplain at the University of Swaziland, and Dr. B. Dlamini, of the Swaziland National Spiritual Assembly of the Baha'i Faith, who read through sections on their respective religions and made useful comments some of which I incorporated in the text. Many thanks go to Dr. Justus Mugaju of Fountain Publishers who read through the manuscript and made useful suggestions to improve on it.

Above all, I wish to express my deep gratitude to my loving wife Vincent and my dear children Charles, Paul, Edgar and Elizabeth for the support and encouragement they gave me in preparation of this book.

May God bless them all.

P.K.

PREFACE

Despite having taught 'Religious Ethics In Africa' at various universities in Uganda, Kenya and Swaziland, for several years, I could not find a book which adequately presents the position of different religions on moral issues nor one that does so from an African perspective. For lecture materials, I depended on primary sources and books of a general nature. It is that material which forms the bulk of this book.

This book is, therefore, an expansion of lectures to my students in Religious Ethics at Kenyatta University, the University of Swaziland and the Institute of Teacher Education, Kyambogo. It is a book on religious ethics in an African context intended to meet the need for a text book in comparative religious ethics. It presents a new approach to the study of ethics in Africa.

The book discusses the teachings of the major religions in Africa, namely African traditional religions, Christianity, Islam and the Baha'i Faith on each of the selected moral issues. Although the different religions have been put side by side giving them equal treatment, the basic position is that, with relevant adjustments to changing situations and circumstances in Africa, the traditional ethic should be recaptured and used as a basis for moral reasoning and decision-making.

It should be noted that when writing about Africa, a continent with many different societies and a variety of cultures, generalisation cannot be avoided. This also applies to Christianity with its various denominations. From time to time, therefore, specific examples are given to minimise this generalisation.

The book is designed to serve as a text book for comparative religious ethics for undergraduate students in universities, teacher training colleges and students in other higher institutions of learning. In addition, it is written in simple, straightforward language in order to be accessible to the general reader.

The approach has been to present the position of each religion on a given moral issue as fairly as possible and in cases where two or more religions have similar positions on an issue, this position is mentioned under each religion. This was done in order to enable the reader who would like to know the position of one particular religion, and not of others, on a particular issue to do so without having to read those of the other religions. Since this is a comparative study, it is rather brief on the stand of each religion on a given issue. Students dealing primarily with ethics from one religious point of view are advised to do further reading on that religion in order to get answers to questions which have not been raised in this book.

The material on each religion was given to the representatives or leaders of the respective religions to read and make their comments. The relevant comments of these people, who are knowledgeable on their respective religions, were incorporated in the text. This means that what is contained in this book is as, much as is humanly possible, a correct and true record of what each religion teaches or prohibits, notwithstanding the variations among groups in each religion.

ITEK, Kyambogo
1998

Chapter One

INTRODUCTION

From the time one wakes up to the time he or she goes to bed, a person is confronted with a multitude of situations in which he or she has to make value decisions and judgements. One decides on what to do and how to do it, and many of these decisions are of a moral nature, requiring a sense of right and wrong; how to do good and avoid evil. If an adult does not have a sense of right and wrong, he or she is counted as insane. Senility, too, may bring about this condition.

Secondly, a person lives and interacts with a variety of people. Social interaction involves making judgements about the character and actions of the people one lives with or encounters. One is expected to act properly and to judge correctly the morality of the actions of other people or institutions he or she interacts with.

One does not, however, arrive at a right moral decision or judgement automatically, as there are no ready made answers to moral problems nor one correct way of doing something in a given situation. Under normal circumstances, one thinks about the problem and then decides. In this process, he or she is guided by the moral value systems of the society. This means that knowledge of these values is important in order to avoid acting or judging in ignorance. A well intentioned person acting in ignorance is likely to err; and affected ignorance, in which a person makes no effort to inform himself or herself, increases blameworthiness for wrong decisions or judgements. It is, therefore, important that one makes reasonable effort to inform oneself, not only of the moral values, but also of ethical guides and theories in order to make informed moral decisions and judgements.

Morality and socialisation
Human beings are social creatures in a sense that they live in communities and learn their behaviour from the groups in which they grow instead of following instinct. Whereas it is true that many animals such as monkeys and chimpanzees acquire certain behavioural traits from observation, animal behaviour is significantly genetically determined. On the other hand, a human being, more than any other being, relies on behaviour patterns, which are learned for survival (Haralambos M, 1985:2). These behaviour patterns, which are necessary for living in the community, are acquired or built up first from the family and then from the larger community.

Right from childhood a person learns the language with which to communicate, the skills with which to cope with the environment, the games played in his or her community, what to eat and when to eat and many other things. Most important of all, he or she learns the social norms that guide her or him on how to relate to other members of the community. A person is expected to use, in the right way, the language, the skills, and the knowledge he or she acquires. This is regulated and controlled by social standards which define what is right or wrong. Thus, an individual's behaviour, purposed and regulated, is different from animal behaviour which is conditioned by instinct. This is called conduct. So over and above instinct, which is the basic disposition to act in an organised way without previous performance, foresight or training, a person develops a second nature which he or she builds up by choice or acquires through experience. The two form a person's character.

This process of socialisation is not limited to childhood. It is a life long process, although the most important stage is from infancy to adolescence. The Banyankore of Uganda aptly have a saying that *akati kainikwa kakiri kabisi* meaning that "a twig is bent while it is still green", or as the English say, "as the twig is bent, so grows the tree".

When a person behaves in the approved or appropriate way he or she is rewarded for it, directly or indirectly. Similarly, disapproved or improper conduct is punishable in a variety of degrees and ways, by the community. Punishments and rewards in the long run become mechanisms for social control and technique to compel members of the group to conform to the norms of the society. This is not to suggest that fear of punishment or the desire for reward are the only motivations for moral behaviour. On the contrary, there are other factors such as religious commitment which lead people to behave 'properly'.

The process of education and socialisation varies from period to period and from society to society. Africa, for example, has witnessed radical changes in the way the members of the various societies on the continent socialise their youth. There are also differences between various African societies as far as moral education is concerned. A general discussion is what is adopted in a study of this nature for a detailed treatment of all the differences would be an impossible task.

Traditional moral education in Africa

Moral education in traditional African societies was a continuous process throughout one's life. This education was both informal and formal. As soon as a baby could understand his or her surroundings, constant effort was made to instil in him or her the proper behaviour for his or her age. The first thing an infant was made to learn are toilet habits. Then when he or she learnt to talk, he or she was taught to greet parents, brothers and sisters, and any person he or she interacted with. He or she was also taught proper sitting posture at meals or in the presence of elders, saying 'thank you' when given something, receiving what is given with both hands, being polite to elders and other approved forms of behaviour. Generally, parents and elders were strict when it came to proper behaviour and character formation of children. Errors in behaviour did not pass uncorrected.

As the child grew to the age of about five years, the parents and elders got more concerned about the cultivation of accepted values of the society in the child. Up to this stage education was informal. The child was always reminded to observe and emulate what older people were doing. Through emulation and participation in home activities, the child acquired certain skills and knowledge appropriate for his or her age and sex. After the age of five or so, vigorous education started. The most common values imparted to children at this stage were respect for elders, generosity, sharing, politeness and being considerate to younger children. As the child grew older, towards puberty, teaching in proper behaviour was intensified, emphasising the virtues imparted at an earlier stage and introducing those which were appropriate for the age. At this stage, a child was usually told things he or she should never do rather than those he or she should do. The vices which were commonly discouraged and prohibited were fornication, betraying one's relatives or friends, stealing and fighting.

A child was not only exposed to family activities. His or her interaction extended to the whole neighbourhood and the clan. Through participation in neighbourhood and clan activities such as weddings, funerals, religious rituals, communal labour and other communal events and activities, a child acquired more knowledge about what was regarded as proper or improper behaviour in that society. This was learning through listening, observation and participation.

Formal education was imparted during the initiation period which took place during adolescence. When the parents and elders observed that the child was ready to become an adult socially and physically, they gave him or her special instructions to prepare him or her for adulthood. This happened just before, or soon after, puberty and it involved more thorough and intensive training and instructions into the ways of the clan or tribe. This, for most societies, was done in a group during the initiation rituals.

Although some African societies did not have elaborate initiation rituals, many others did. These rituals, which varied from society to society, introduced a young person into adulthood. The young men and women were secluded from society for a period during which they received instructions about adult life and proper behaviour for adults. Even in societies without institutionalised initiation rites, at puberty, the girls and boys received instructions from the parents or aunts and uncles about proper behaviour in adult life. This process of instruction was completed just before marriage. After marriage, men and women continued to learn proper behaviour through participation in communal activities and guidance from the elders.

Africa's changing patterns

Unlike in the past when children associated with their parents and relatives, learning from them, nowadays children grow up in schools. There has also been the process of urbanisation and many children grow up in towns with their working parents. Thus, they are not able to observe or to participate in clan or wider community functions. Even those children who grow up in rural areas, but have been converted to foreign religions, are often prohibited by their new religions to participate in traditional functions and rituals. Age groups, which brought together the youths of the same age, are also disappearing. With the influence of Western education and foreign religions such as Christianity, Islam and the Baha'i Faith, the standards of behaviour that used to guide the youths in moral decision making, have also changed. Because several religions, each with its own ethics, were intermingled, a new breed of morality has emerged.

In order to maintain their identity, it is imperative for Africans to rediscover their heritage, especially the African ethics embedded in African religions and use it as the starting point in moral revaluation.

Scope and contents

This book is designed to serve as an introduction to a comparative study of religious ethics in Africa. After the theoretical discourse in Chapter Two, a number of moral issues in Africa, focusing on individual morality, are examined and discussed. As a matter of fact, the boundary between individual and social morality is a fluid one as an individual's actions, to some extent, influence others and sometimes the whole community for good or for ill. Nevertheless, a distinction can be made between those moral issues which have to do mainly with the individual and those which mainly concern groups of people or whole societies.

Whereas beating one's wife, for example, is an individual act of violence with moral implications, war is clearly a social one. So while individual morality is about person to person relations, social morality deals with those issues which are primarily of a group nature and can only be undertaken by such a group, though of course the individuals may influence group morality by their participation in its activities, decision making and, in some cases, by protest and resistance.

Social morality applies to large-scale social structures such as whole nations or societies. It can also apply either to more local levels such as a clan, town, district and province or to international relations. Social moral problems thus lie more in the economic, social, political, ecological, communication and international spheres while individual morality situated more in personal conduct.

Between individual and social morality is family morality. Family moral issues and decisions concern both personal integrity and the welfare of the individual in the domestic framework of the whole family as a group. The family moral issues are closer to individuals than they are to social issues and will, therefore, be discussed in this book. In view of the above, special attention is given to issues related to life and death, sexuality, marriage and family life.

An attempt is made to reflect on each moral issue from the vantage point different religious perspectives. Since Africa is a religiously plural society, it is proper that this study should reflect that religious pluralism. The constant contact and interactions between people with different religious beliefs and practices, which influence society, makes it necessary to take note, try to understand, reflect upon and sometimes to apply religious ethics of another religion in a given social context. Hence, the importance of the study of this nature.

In each of the religions covered by this book, there are sectarian or denominational differences on certain issues which at times are not consistent with each other. Even in each denomination members disagree on answers to some of the moral questions confronted. An attempt has, therefore, been made to present the most representative view of each religion. Inevitably, this means that some people may not wholly agree with what is presented as a true reflection of their religion's position on a given issue.

Secularism in Africa is also a force to be reckoned with. Along with industrialisation, technology, education, entertainment, legal systems and all the other aspects of Western culture, which Africans have been eager to adopt, come secular values. Secular principles and rationality are a powerful influence on people's ethical values almost everywhere in Africa today. This is an aspect that cannot be ignored.

The aim of this book is not to defend one ethical system against another or to show the superiority of one of them over others, rather it is to describe, as accurately as possible, the alternative religious ethical systems on the continent in order to understand them better. The approach of this book is neither apologetic, advocatory nor normative. It is rather descriptive and comparative, based on the available information. An individual, in a concrete situation, should work out his or her own autonomous position on the moral issue in question. This book only provides resources to draw from and tools to use in doing so.

An important resource, however, remains the African heritage. Whether one is a Muslim, Christian or a Baha'i, he or she is first and foremost an African, interacting with Africans. It is this Africanness that gives one his or her identity and provides him or her with the sense of belonging and meaning of life, shared and realised in the well-being of the community. In terms of morality African traditions have a lot to offer. The African value of communalism, with its emphasis on mutual concern, respect for seniority and consideration for juniors, generosity, honesty, hospitality, the high regard for the transmission and preservation of life, the sacredness of sex, the importance attached to marriage and family life, the concern for the poor, orphans, widows and strangers, and the high value attached to children, is a good base for moral living.

African values were undermined and to some extent disrupted by cultural influences from the West and the East as well as the social changes induced by industrialisation and urbanisation. Throughout this book it will be emphasised that in order to overcome the individualism, materialism and lack of concern for the welfare of others which are the cause of most moral problems in Africa to-day, an attempt should be made to rediscover African moral values and use them as the starting point in moral decision-making and judgement.

The book is divided into nine chapters. Chapter One, the Introduction, discusses the value of morals for the individual and for the society and their role in the process of socialisation.

Chapter Two discusses ethics in general and covers the definitions of ethics and morals, guides to moral decision-making and moral theories and principles.

Chapter Three specifically discusses religion and ethics in Africa and examines the basis of ethics for each of the four religions mentioned above.

The following four chapters examine specific moral issues. Chapter four discusses life and death issues relating to the preservation and promotion of one's life. The issues discussed are drug abuse, smoking, alcoholism and suicide. Chapter Five focuses on life and death issues concerning respect for other people's lives. The issues discussed are assault and homicide, violence in self-defence, abortion, euthanasia and wife-beating.

Chapter Six covers sex outside marriage. It discusses sexual ethics in general and goes on to discuss fornication, adultery, prostitution, homosexuality, masturbation, and sexism. Chapter Seven discusses marriage and covers celibacy and the duty to marry, choice of marriage partner, polygamy, divorce and bride-gifts exchange. Chapter eight is on family life. It discusses the emerging family patterns, the status of women in the home and in public, the status of children and family planning. The final chapter focuses on moral responsibility and the components of a moral act.

For each moral issue discussed, there is a brief introduction explaining the concepts and introducing the main arguments involved. Then the position of each of the four religions on the topic is described. This is followed by concluding remarks in which an attempt is made to make a synthesis of what has been covered. Each moral issue is discussed as an independent unit so that a reader interested in one, and not another, issue can read and understand it without difficulty.

Chapter Two

ETHICAL THEORY

It is proper and necessary to start the discussion on religious ethics by defining the main terms used in this book namely ethics and morals. This is because a clear understanding of the nomenclature used is important for a smooth sailing through the book.

Ethics and morality are terms that are often used interchangeably perhaps because they are closely related. Etymologically, ethics is derived from the Greek word *ethos* which refers to the characteristic values, beliefs and practices of a social group. An ethos is constituted by the pervasive beliefs and values that are seldom questioned within a given society.

Morality, on the other hand, is derived from a Latin word, *mores* which also refers to customs or the generally held beliefs and practices of a given society. *Mores* are the social norms of a given society making its moral system. By a moral system is meant the integrated and systematised set of ideas of right and wrong in a given culture which regulate individual moral judgements and social morality. So both *ethos* and *mores* mean the habits or customs of a people by which a given community lives.

Nevertheless, this does not mean that ethics and morality are exactly the same thing. Broadly speaking, ethics refers to a systematic and thematic discipline, a set of principles which may be used to criticise or evaluate norms such as customs or laws that regulate the way of life of people in a given community, while morality refers to the implementation of those principles or the disposition one has (Curran C, 1982:82). So, whereas ethics refers to principles of behaviour, morality refers to behaviour itself. In short, ethics is a reflection on morality; its nature, its presuppositions and its applications.

Ethics apply to all human activities in which actions of one person or group(s) affect the well being of others. The complexity of human situations, varying from individual to world scale activities, complicates ethical issues and moral decisions. There are, therefore, various forms of ethics such as business ethics, medical ethics, environmental ethics and legal ethics. Technological advances in medicine and industry have also complicated the moral scene further and introduced new and more complicated ethical branches of ethics such as bio-ethics.

Ethics as a study
As an academic study ethics is a branch of philosophy which is concerned with principles of morality and theories about what is considered right or wrong,

good or evil, in people's conduct. It is a philosophy dealing with ordinary questions such as what is a morally right action?, what human values or goals are to be realised? who is a good person? and the answers to those questions.

The study of ethics may be undertaken in order to do three things. The first one is to prescribe normative moral criteria for justifying rules and judgements of what is morally right or wrong, good or evil or how people ought to behave. This is normative ethics. The normative task of ethics is "to propose norms, standards, rules or principles to guide us in our moral and our judgements (choices or priorities)" (Ratanakul P, 1986: 25). Normative ethics proposes guides for action and principles that constitute the basis for moral judgements. They are intended to help humanity to decide wisely, and not to act in ignorance, foolishness, prejudice or in sheer wilful perversity and self-deception. Religious ethics is one form of normative ethics.

Another reason to study ethics may be to analyse the language and meanings of moral concepts and of the methods of supporting moral arguments. This is meta-ethics. The analytical task of meta-ethics consists mainly in raising questions about the meaning of ethical language. It also seeks reasons to justify, for example, calling one action right and another wrong, one thing good and another one bad. It is an attempt to establish rational defence or foundation for moral values and judgements. Whereas normative ethics provides theories about what ought to be done, meta-ethics gives theories about what ethics is all about"(Reich W, 1978: 403). Ethics may also be studied to describe and compare the answers given by particular societies or groups to the questions of right or wrong conduct in order to understand them. This is comparative ethics which is the main concern of this book.

Guides to moral decision-making

Often a person is confronted with situations in which he or she has to make a moral decision. At times this is not easy, especially when everything seems to be called into question or two or more values seem to conflict. The basic moral principle is that "good is to be done and evil to be avoided". It is said that the morally good is that which ought to be done and the morally evil is what ought not to be done. The question, however, is how does a person know what is morally good or morally evil? because at times they are not obvious.

Internal guides

When confronted with a situation that entails making a moral decision, a person may rely on internal guides; either on feelings, intuition, reason or conscience for guidance. Each of these may lead a person to act correctly, but since none of them is infallible, following their guidance could lead to a wrong decision.

In a situation where a moral decision is based on feelings, it becomes extremely subjective. When a person says "it feels good, therefore, I will do it", he or she is making an extreme subjective decision. This can be very dangerous in moral matters of marriage, friendship, business or office responsibilities.

Another subjective, but more acceptable tool in moral decision-making, is intuition. Every normal person with a sound mind has an inner feeling, an immediate direct perception or insight of the state of affairs which guides him or her when faced with a situation that requires immediate response or action. This is an innate moral sense, in normal persons, to do good and to avoid evil. It is a direct and often spontaneous insight which is gained naturally and through experience and depends on one's level of intelligence. From this, a "moral fact" theory has developed. According to this theory, some moral truths, at least the basic ones, are self-evident like other facts or truths. For example, everyone knows that life is better than death, truth is better than falsehood, love is better than hatred and pleasure is better than pain. From these truths, moral positions can be worked out on how to treat others in concrete situations and how to conduct oneself.

However, intuition is only helpful in situations requiring quick and immediate action. In situations where a person has adequate time to decide on the course of action, intuition is not an adequate guide because there is no evidence to show that this innate moral sense is consistent and reliable. So, although intuition is important, it is too subjective and, therefore, too relative to be helpful on social issues. It can be of great help on private and individual moral decisions, but not on issues of public policy. Even in personal matters reason seems to be a better guide.

A healthy person has reasoning capacity for assessing situations rationally and for ethical reflection. This means that a person is capable of making moral decisions based on facts, knowledge of the moral principles, and after a logical analysis and process. Reason helps a person to make an orderly and thoughtful approach to the problem to which one applies general moral principles before deciding on what to do. This is the guide that seems to be most appropriate before taking a decision on serious moral issues such as abortion, or euthanasia. However, reason, too, may be subjective and that is why people often disagree so much on moral issues such as abortion, homosexuality, racial intermarriage, or the treatment of animals.

Between intuition and reason, is conscience. Conscience is the common moral sense of right or wrong which any normal person has and which is used to deliberate on moral action in order to discover the right thing to do in a given situation. It is what is often called the 'inner voice', 'the heart', or 'the voice of God' which is an inner sense that helps a person to decide, when faced with moral decision-making. In Christian terms, conscience is often referred to as the Holy Spirit or guardian angel. It is the 'higher law' which many people respond to and even, at times, leads them to disobey institutionalised laws.

Conscience is not an independent guide by itself either. It is a product of conditioning and is shaped by a person's family, upbringing and society. As a guide, it is less spontaneous than intuition and draws from experience, reason and moral tradition. Like intuition, conscience is valuable as a moral guide only in private and personal matters, not in public issues as no one can live by another person's conscience.

As to whether conscience can be wrong, the answer is 'yes'. Conscience can err because it can be corrupted by personal, social, or economic interests. It may also make errors of factual judgement, because of ignorance and, therefore, failing to be sensitive enough to the personal or social factors involved in the issues at stake. There are also situations when it errs by wrongly estimating the possible consequences of some actions in deciding what to do (Childress J, 1986:116).

Following one's conscience, therefore, does not exonerate a person from blameworthiness because if serious decisions are taken lightly, judgements are made on the basis of insufficient information, or when there is a failure to consult appropriate authorities in complex situations, conscience may decide erroneously. The person in each of these cases is responsible for his or her actions. Besides, a person who constantly refuses to listen to his or her conscience can blunt its sensitivity to moral values or condition it in illegitimate ways. So the conscience to which one can appeal, is one which is continually self-critical and is aware of the dangers of ignorance, bias, prejudice, selfishness, arrogance and self-sufficiency (Komonchak J.A, 1988:229). If it is well informed and instructed by external guides, conscience remains one's ultimate guide.

External guides

Because of the inadequacy of subjective internal guides, people have to resort to external guides for deciding on what is right or wrong. These may be persons or rules, and they may be secular or religious. Authoritative people include parents, teachers, police, civil leaders, philosophers and religious leaders. Guidance may also be given by rules whether codified or not. There are several sets of moral rules which are imparted to a person through a group he or she belongs to. These sets of rules prescribe what is right or wrong and are often a justification for a person's actions. Usually, the first external guide a person resorts to, even without thinking, is custom. Every society has its customs which are the approved norms and ways of doing things and which shape the people's response to the normal conditions of life, interpersonal relationships and the environment in which they live. Customary morality is based on tradition, the way things have always been done either in the family, community or whole societies. Custom prescribes action or non-action and may eventually be formulated into law or taboos when greater sanction is required to keep it from being changed. Under customary morality, right behaviour is determined by those forms of conduct which are approved by the standards of inherited modes of behaviour of the social group to which one belongs. Customary morality is maintained, among other things, by public opinion, taboos, religious sanctions and rituals, and sometimes by the fear of either physical force or magic.

In changing circumstances, however, a person may find it difficult to abide by customs and will rely on other sources of guidance, such as religion or the law for his conduct. In traditional societies, customary ethical laws are inseparable from religion, but in other societies, custom, religion and law are separate though they may be related in many ways. Religion is an external guide that is discussed at length in this book.

The internal and external guides can be mutually exclusive in the sense that what is right or wrong is determined exclusively either by reason, conscience, custom, law or revelation. On the other hand, they can be complementary. Revelation, for example, can supplement reason reducing the possibility of error and giving new duties arising from the new knowledge which is above the power of reason to acquire. Thus, revelation can facilitate the general dissemination of what reason can acquire only with difficulty and in a few people. Reason, too, may be necessary for interpreting or understanding revelation. Similarly, custom and law can assist revealed morality by making it known and observed. However, law and custom are only moral when what they prescribe is good in itself: not those acts which are only good because they are prescribed and the contrary might be good or bad depending on nature of law or custom.

Although conscience is not infallible and a good person can be guilty of self-deception, still it remains the supreme guide for a person. When a well-informed and well-developed conscience clashes with an external guide, whether civil, customary or ecclesiastical, a person is obliged to follow his or her conscience. Conscience, more than any other guide brings together the whole person; reason, feeling, experience and knowledge while passing a moral judgement.

Moral theories
Intuition, reason and conscience are subjective moral guides while custom, religion and law are relative and apply to members of that society, religion or nation. The usefulness of the two guides, therefore, is not necessarily universal. Philosophers have attempted to establish universal objective grounds free from subjectivism or relativism for deciding on what is right or wrong. Several moral theories have been put forward to do this.

Teleological theories
The term 'teleological' comes from a Greek word *telos* which means end. According to teleological ethics, the moral quality of an act is determined by its end results such as usefulness, happiness, prosperity and pleasure. There is nothing right or wrong in any act itself, but in what follows from it. One of the teleological theories is utilitarianism according to which the rightness of an act is measured by the amount of good over evil, the amount of pleasure over pain and the amount of happiness over the distress it produces.

The basic principle in utilitarian ethics is that people ought, in all circumstances, to do what, of all possible alternative actions, will produce the greatest value for all the people affected by their actions, with everyone's good counting equally (Ratanakul P, 1986:65). It advocates the "greatest good for the greatest number". On a personal level, utilitarianism advocates the view that one ought to do what is in one's best interests. This may not be immediate pleasure or happiness, but enlightened long term self-interest.

Many people find principles embedded in teleological ethics appealing for pragmatic judgement. However, others find teleological theories strange, especially those who hold the view that moral judgement should be as categorical and unconditional as possible so that they do not lose their force. Another criticism of this theory is that people rarely agree on categorising what is good. Whereas some would, for example, choose freedom, others would choose comfort, convenience, pleasure, independence, security or any other related value.

When these values conflict, people disagree on how to rank them. In euthanasia, for example, it is not easy to tell what occupies a higher value between continued life or freedom from pain. In situations when a person cannot have two values such as independence and security in old age, which one takes priority becomes a problem.

Another problem is related to quantifying the weight of good over evil. How much pain, for example, for a person who wants to commit suicide, is greater evil than continued life, or how much pleasure will justify the risk of death for those who go to night clubs? In all these issues, the decision is private and in public matters it is at times difficult to apply this theory.

Justice also becomes an issue in situations where the good of one person or of a section conflicts with the good of another group. A good example is a woman wanting to commit abortion against the will of her husband or family. Another example is how to equitably balance the rights or interests of the minority with those of the majority. This happens, for example, in political or religious issues. Even in ideal democracies it is not fair to ignore the interests or good of the minority.

Deontological theories

Deontological theories differ fundamentally from teleological ones. Deontological theories emphasise duty. Etymologically, the term comes from a Greek word *deon* which means what is obligatory or necessary. According to deontological ethics, some things are right and others are wrong to do by their very nature and one has the obligation to do what is right irrespective of its consequences and to avoid what is wrong no matter what happens to him or her. Deontological ethics rests on the social nature of humanity and on the reciprocity of rights and obligations. Deontologists believe that individuals have a "social contract" with everyone in society in ever widening circles of family, community, clan, nation, and, finally, of mankind.

In these circles, one finds social ties and relationships of kinship, friendship, profession or marriage. In these relationships, some contracts are formally spelled out, as the marriage, business and professional contracts, others are just understood as in the family, the relationship between children and parents, or in the community as a whole. These social relationships determine obligations between members and these obligations are a basis for moral action. Fidelity to promises, gratitude for benefits received, truthfulness, and justice are some of the things deontologists point out as right to do, no matter what happens.

There are some deontologists who are not interested in rules, but would allow the obligations of each case to dictate what is right, but the majority of them are "rule deontologists". According to rule deontologists, the standards of obligation are expressed in rules or principles, some very specific as in the Ten Commandments and others quite general as in 'love God and your neighbour'.

The natural law theory

One of the most controversial theories in ethics is the natural law theory. According to the natural law theory, the way the world is ordered and runs shows that people should act in conformity with natural law, not contrary to it. The basic idea is that any person who carefully studies human nature and who reflects upon it, will be able to discover natural laws of human moral behaviour.

Such laws, because they are based on the order of things and can be discovered by anyone, should be universal and binding on all humanity.

The concept of natural law gives rise to the concept of natural rights. According to natural rights, people enter society with certain inalienable rights just by virtue of being human, regardless of what they do. These rights are not based on the social contract, but they are inherently human. Rights of men, women, children, minority groups and even of animals are based on natural law. Written laws according to the natural law theory, should never contradict natural laws, but draw from them.

In Christian terms, natural law is the law of God imprinted in man. This is the law St. Paul refers to when he argues, "Ever since God created the world, his invisible qualities, both his eternal power and his divine nature, have been clearly seen; they are perceived in the things that God has made. So those people have no excuse at all!" (Rom. I:18-21). He also talks of the law that is written on the hearts of people (Rom. 2: 14-16). This view also appears in Acts 17:23ff.

The world, according to this view, reveals God's plan and purpose for people and the world. People should follow it. The argument is that the world was created by God, who intended it to operate in a certain way and when people go against nature, they go against God. Deliberate interference with natural order, too, is regarded as wrong because God did not intend it to operate that way (Rom. 1:26; I Cor. 11:14; Human Vitae, : 5-13). The church uses the natural law argument on the ethics of abortion, sex, contraceptives, homosexuality and other moral issues.

Some churches, however, are sceptical of the ability of mankind to conform to natural law because of the fall of man and they emphasise revelation to supplement and enlighten it. Others emphasise a third source of moral knowledge, namely the church law or tradition. The argument being that revelation requires interpretation and the church, with its history, experience and institutions, is the best organisation to do so. In the history of the church, the Roman Catholic church, the reformers such as Martin Luther and John Calvin and many other theologians have upheld the principles of natural law while others have argued against its applicability (Wogaman J.P, 1976: 7-8).

Even in secular terms, the principle of beneficence and non-maleficence, and their associated demands of kindness, mercy, generosity, compassion, goodness, and love, are based on natural law.

Situation ethics
Another group of ethical theories is situation ethics. According to situation ethical reasoning the basic measure of rightness of an act is not intrinsic to the

act nor is it a function of its consequences. Whether something is right or wrong depends on the uniqueness of the situation; whether or not it is appropriate to do in a given situation. The circumstances in which one finds himself or herself will determine the course of his or her actions rather than following moral rules and principles.

In contrast to deontological and to some extent consequential systems which tend to establish sets of rules to guide individuals, situation ethics does not value rules highly. Situation ethicists tend to agree that there are no universally applicable rules that provide a basis for moral judgement (Wogaman J.P, 1976: 15). The ethical laws and principles, scriptures, tradition, and moral theories are accepted as guides rather than prescription. According situation ethics "the agent has to discern what should be done in the immediate situation without relying on intermediate rules to connect that principle to the situation" (Childress J, 1986: 586).

Opponents of situation ethics criticise it on several grounds. First of all, they do not see situation ethics as only being antinomianism but see it as being anti-law. It is also often pointed out that because of human shortcomings and weaknesses, many people are not able to discern right action or to calculate, predict or control the consequences of their actions (Childress J, 1986 : 586). Situation ethics requires that a person is well informed and is of sound mind. Besides, there are many people in society who may not use that freedom responsibly, who need controlling sanctions. Situation ethics is also criticised for being too individualistic, especially in Africa where the community spirit is still very strong.

Chapter Three

RELIGION, ETHICS AND MORALITY

It is commonly held that religion and morality are inseparable, morality being part of religion. Some people even go as far as saying that religion and morality are one and the same thing; as religion is expected to be one's way of life. It is thus often said that if there was no threat of hell, at least as far as Christians and Muslims are concerned, people would do all sorts of evil. Others argue that without belief in God, gods, or ancestors, even if it is not for fear of hell, there would be no reason for being good. (Tremmel W, 1984:232) God's will or the will of ancestors creates moral standards. These views associate morality very closely with religion.

Other people, however, tend to separate religion and morality arguing that the two are distinct, and morality may be non-religious. In fact, an extreme view is to advocate a non-religious morality. This point deserves elaboration.

In concrete terms, most religions have a way of conduct which is regarded as right and proper for their adherents. This is expressed in moral rules which the adherents are required to keep. In fact, most religions stipulate the guides which followers must comply with in relation to one another and to humanity in general. They prescribe what is right or wrong conduct, who is a good or bad person and what is a good or bad life. Morality is regarded as one way adherents of a religion use to please the God they worship, to live in harmony within the community and to enjoy blessings from above.

However, not all forms of morality have a religious connection. At times, religion and morality do not require or prohibit the same conduct. The two may even demand conflicting way of behaviour, especially in a society with religions which spread from outside Africa. This was, for example, the case when Christianity came to Africa and put demands which conflicted with African ethical values. So whereas religious and moral requirements may overlap, this may not always be the case. Essentially, religion is about what one's God, gods or ancestors demand or desire while morality is about what is beneficial or harmful to human beings or their environment.

In morality, certain forms of behaviour are recommended or prohibited not because religion does not permit them, but because society does not accept them (Tremmel W, 1984:232). Thus, morality does not necessarily depend on religion for it can depend on reason, natural law or other secular guides. Though religion and morality are not always the same, they are often related and influence each other and even overlap in many ways in a given society. When the two are similar, as it happens in most cases, moral values receive divine sanction and turn into religious ethics.

At other times, morality influences religion to change it. An aspect of religious ethics which is common to all the four religions that are discussed in this book is authoritarianism. Each religion has its moral rules which it regards as an infallible guide to proper behaviour for its adherents. These rules are regarded as God's or ancestors' commands which are beyond questioning. Everyone is expected to obey them with or without understanding or agreeing with them. Whoever does not follow them is regarded as immoral and, therefore, deserving punishment from above or from the religious community, itself.

Religion and morality in Africa
In any African society, religion plays an important role in people's conduct. It is the strongest force that unites people into community and gives individuals a sense of identity. Ancestors control both individual and social morals.

In modern Africa, the religious scene is complicated. Instead of one religious system of meaning, there are several religions, at times with conflicting moral value positions on some issues. There are many religions in Africa, but in terms of numbers the main ones are African religions, Christianity, Islam and the Baha'i Faith. This book focuses on these religions.

African religions
Africans are very religious people and religion constitutes their way of life, influencing their physical, material, social or political concerns. All individual and group activities are religiously determined. At the same time, religion presents a corporate religiosity in the sense that it is not clearly differentiated from other modes of beliefs and behaviour. It embraces the total life of the people and is integrated in all their institutions. The religious and the secular interpenetrate, to a greater or lesser degree, at all points of existence. In whatever an African does or experiences, there is a simultaneous working of spiritual and worldly forces. Thus, one cannot separate religion from morality.

However, exceptions are beginning to emerge, and African religions are continually being eroded by the foreign religions due to the latter's aggressive propaganda. Nevertheless, the influence of African religions on the people is still strong, especially among those people who did not accept the other three religions and among members of Christian independent churches. Traditional values, beliefs and practices, especially ethical ones, continue to be revered and manifested in almost all spheres of life and to co-exist with modern values and values of the other three religions, producing an interesting and complex mixture.

Christianity

Christianity first came to Africa in the first century AD, during the apostolic period. Starting from Egypt, it spread to Sudan and later to Ethiopia. Although it did not spread farther at this time, in the fifteenth and sixteenth centuries, Christianity spread to almost all coastal areas of the continent. Towards the end of the eighteenth century, freed Christian slaves returning to Africa, carried Christianity further into the interior, but with limited expansion. Perhaps the most successful period of Christian spread in Africa was the nineteenth and twentieth centuries, the so-called 'missionary period'. It is during this period when Christianity penetrated into the continent, expanding and exerting tremendous influence on the converts.

From missionary Christianity sprang indigenous churches which either seceded from the mother churches or were born as a result of a 'calling' to the founder. Several factors, including moral ones such as racial discrimination, economic deprivation and political oppression, contributed to the rise of these churches. The main factor, in many cases, however, was culture. Due to cultural imperialism, most missionaries wanted "to uproot the African, body and soul, from his old customs and beliefs, put him in a class by himself, with all tribal traditions shattered and his institutions trampled upon" (Kenyatta, 1938: 269-70). This did not work well. Many Africans broke off from missionary churches and founded their own churches where they integrated the positive elements of their culture with the Christian ones. This enabled them to reject Western moral values such as polygamy which were not acceptable to them.

After some time, even in mission founded churches, a process of contexualisation emerged attempting to express Christianity in the 'language' of the people; incarnating the gospel which meant taking seriously the people's cultural values, history, experience and their future. This meant rediscovering positive African values, including moral ones, and integrating them into the new Christian ethos.

Islam

Of the religions which came to Africa, Islam claims the biggest number of followers. Within a year after the death of Prophet Mohammed, its founder, in AD 632, Islam occupied a big part of North Africa. It continued to penetrate the continent, especially West Africa, Sudan, and the East African coast, through trade contacts. As Arab trade extended farther into the interior, Islam penetrated the continent.

Islamic ethics has a lot in common with African ethical values, especially in terms of sex and marriage, and this makes conversion to Islam by Africans easier. However, the two differ in some other areas such as matters of dietary laws and alcoholic consumption.

The Baha'i Faith
The latest of the revealed religions of the world is the Baha'i Faith. From the time it was established in 1863, the Faith has rapidly spread to all corners of the world and claims millions of followers. It is not only the youngest of the world religions, it is also different from them. For example, it recognises and respects all the religions revealed before it, stresses the oneness of all religions, and works for the attainment of world peace and the unity of mankind.

The Baha'i Faith was first introduced to Africa by the founder's son, Abdul Baha, in 1911, when he made a teaching tour of Egypt and West African countries (Mbiti J, 1969:260). It is in the 1950's, however, when the Faith spread to most African countries. The headquarters of the Faith, in Africa, are in Kampala, Uganda.

The Baha'i Faith teaches the oneness of God, religion and mankind, preaches brotherhood, justice, equal rights and privileges of all people and harmony between religion and science while condemning prejudice, slavery, asceticism, ignorance, exploitation and oppression, and advocates compulsory education, elimination of poverty, sex within marriage and obedience to one's government. These and many others of its social teachings are acceptable to many people in Africa, educated and uneducated. The Faith, therefore, exerts considerable influence on the morality of its followers and on society generally.

The basics of religious ethics
Having briefly described the four main religions in Africa it is necessary to briefly discuss the basics of their ethics beginning with African traditional religions. Writing about an aspect of African life creates a number of problems. For example, Africans are not a monolithic society. Africa, being a home of about 1000 different peoples, with different value systems and cultures (Mbiti J, 1969:101) is a diverse and complex contintent of. It means, therefore, that it is difficult to avoid generalisation. Besides, there are sub-cultures emerging, for example, an urban sub-culture, the 'educated' sub-culture and several other sub-cultures, with variations in ethical values. Nevertheless, despite variety, there is a common Africanness about the totality of African culture and world view which will serve as the basis discussion in this book.

African traditional morality is expressed through custom which consists of rules, laws, and taboos which are handed down from generation to generation. According to customary morality, a person is expected to behave in compliance with the established behavioural patterns of the group which are acquired through the process of socialisation.

In Africa, customary morality is stronger in small traditional societies, such as the Swazi who are political, economic and religious unities, but it is also still widespread, to a lesser degree, in pluralistic societies. Whereas it has many advantages and is extremely functional in ordering society, customary morality has a number of defects such as openness to 'superstitions', treating petty matters as equally important or even more important than great ones, too much rigidity, too limited individual freedom and initiative and several others.

In African societies strong emphasis is put on community and one's relationship with others. Consequently, the solidarity of the community must be maintained and many laws, rites, observances and taboos exist which constitute the moral code of the community and enhance communalism. Breach of this code of behaviour is considered evil, wrong or bad because it is a destruction to the acceptable social order and peace. Moral evil is what a person does against his or her fellow human beings. Thus, in African societies, immorality is the word or deed which undermines fellowship. What strengthens the life of the community is right and what weakens it is evil, and therefore wrong.

The basic philosophy behind African morality is the belief in ancestors who are the authority of the living elders and rulers. It is believed that society morals were given to the people by God through the ancestors. This provides authority which cannot be challenged easily. The common belief is that ancestors keep watch over people to make sure that they observe the morals, to punish those who violate them and to reward the people when they conform. This is done in order to preserve the welfare of the community.

Since the morals of each society are embedded in their customs, rituals, beliefs and practices, people assimilate them as they grow up and participate in the community in which they live.

Christian ethics are varied. There are hundreds of Christian denominations, with a variety of ethical positions on the application of the fundamental Christian ethical principles to particular problems. There is thus, no homogeneous Christian ethical system to talk about. Despite variety, however, it is possible to identify the basic Christian ethical principles and even positions on moral issues which justify talking about Christian ethics. In this book the approach to Christian ethics will be a general one, focusing on the basic features and principles which are common to all, or to at least most of the denominations, and which distinguish Christian ethics from other religions' ethics. Except where necessary, the moral positions of particular churches will be discussed.

Christian ethics, like any form of religious ethics, is concerned with both the relationship between people and the relationship between people and ultimate reality. In personal matters, Christian ethics does not put a sharp line between a person's relationship with God and his or her relationship with neighbours. The basic Christian principles of personal ethics are found in the

Bible and the church tradition. A Christian is expected to serve God and to perform righteousness (Rom.6:13). Although the believer is free from the Old Testament law as a means of gaining salvation, he or she is under the law of Christ (1 Cor 9:21) through whom the will of God was made known to humanity.

Christ's basic moral principle on which all other rules and commandments stand is the double commandment of love; to love God wholly and to love one's neighbour as self. Jesus himself set this principle (Mt. 22:37-40). Like the principle of 'Do good and avoid evil' the above commandment, however, is very general and both revelation and reason contribute to deciding on how to love. This commandment is rooted in the Old Testament commandments (Ex. 20: 1-17). Jesus elaborated on them to give them deeper meaning and the apostles interpreted them for their followers. The different churches continue to interpret them and the law of love, and to relate them to the context in which Christians live in order to guide their conduct. Churches also continue to break down the law of love to give specific details as situations arise.

A basic difference among Christian churches is how to discover God's will when it comes to details and specifics. Fundamentalist groups insist on the literal understanding of God's revealed will in the Bible. Mainline Protestant churches emphasise the personal relation between an individual with God and thus, over and above Scriptures, they advocate using one's intellect and consulting one's conscience. The Roman Catholic church, arguing that Scriptures require competent interpretation and that consciences differ and conscience is not always reliable especially when it is not well informed, teach that the church is the vicar of God on earth and is the channel to communicate God's will and to interpret the Bible for the followers.

Islam has divine law and a scheme of moral values to guide Muslims in life. All aspects of a Muslims's life are regulated by religious law which covers almost all aspects of life. A Muslim is instructed on how to eat, dress, slaughter animals, clean one's body, do business, work, participate in government or deal with his wife or her husband. All areas of private and public conduct are regulated by religion.

In concrete situations, a Muslim's first guide is the Quran. When a Muslim does not get guidance from the Quran, he or she tries the traditions of Muhammad known as *Hadith*. Prophet Muhammad is described in the Quran as "a beautiful pattern (of conduct)" (33:21) and one who stands "On an exalted standard of character" (68:4). So he is taken as the model of good conduct and the best interpreter of the Quran. His actions (sunna) and statements (hadith) are followed by Muslims in every detail. The narratives of his actions, words and silent approval on a range of subjects were recorded in Hadith and constitute a guide for a Muslim's conduct.

The other guide to a Muslim is the Sharia. Sharia means 'clear path' and it is the path which leads one into submission to Allah. It contains laws for Muslims to follow in all aspects of life, privately and publicly. Its prescriptions for Muslims include things that are obligatory (*farrah*), recommended (*sunnah*), legally indifferent and, therefore, permitted (*mubah*), discouraged (*makruh*), or prohibited (*haram*). The Sharia is based on three things namely the Quran, the Hadith and the traditions of the early Muslims. If these three fail to provide specific guidance on an issue, the muslim scholars and doctors of the law rely on consensus of the community (*ijma*) and on analogical reasoning (*qiyas*) to determine the muslim moral position on that issue.

The general principle in Islam is that all things which were created by God, and the benefits derived from them, are essentially good and for people to use and hence are permissible. Nothing is bad except what God has prohibited. This is the principle of 'natural usability and permissibility' which is based on the Quran (31:20).

The Baha'i Faith is a religion that emphasises unity and peaceful mutual co-existence. Proper conduct is, therefore, a highly stressed value. Baha'u'llah himself wrote:

> Fear God, O people, and refrain from shedding the blood of any one. Contend not with your neighbor, and be ye of them that do good. Beware that ye commit no disorders on the earth after it hath been well ordered, and follow not the footsteps of them that are gone astray. (Baha'u'llah, 1976:277)

The Bab, who came before Baha'u'llah, called upon his followers to be distinguished by brotherly love and courtesy, to grant women fuller freedom, to provide for the poor, not to use intoxicating drinks and to live a life of entire devotion to God and to the service of others. Love was a central value of his teaching.

Abdul Baha, who came after Baha'u'llah, too, emphasised love for one another and called upon Baha'is to be "as one soul in many bodies for the more we love each other, the nearer we shall be to God" (Tablets of Abdul Baha, vol. 1, p. 147). According to the Baha'i Faith it, is through humanity that one can get nearer to God and if one turns his or her back to his or her fellow human beings, he or she is turning it upon God. Consequently, the Baha'i Faith emphasises praiseworthy moral behaviour as the surest evidence of spiritual growth.

In the following chapters, specific moral issues will be discussed focusing on the position of each of the four religions.

The point of departure between African religions ethics and the ethics of the three religions which came to Africa is that whereas the three emphasise an individualistic doctrine of salvation, the African ethic is communalistic. The three religions emphasise individuality and individual responsibility to God, but the African ethic advocates corporate existence and responsibility; to be is to belong. Without necessarily undermining individual autonomy, the book advocates a return, where possible, to the African world view. It is this world view which was potential for community and unity of humanity.

Chapter Four

THE PRESERVATION AND PROMOTION OF ONE'S LIFE

Perhaps the greatest value for any human being is one's life and the greatest duty is to preserve and promote its wholeness. This value is universally recognised. According to the Universal Declaration of Human Rights, for example, "Everyone has the right to life, liberty and security of person" (Article 3). This is a fundamental human right which no one may threaten or deprive of another person without justifiable reasons.

The basic question which is addressed in this chapter is: has a person got a right to take his or her own life or to do with his or her body whatever he or she likes? Whereas there are many people who would say "yes" many more would argue that living is not only a right but also a duty. This implies the duty to cherish, protect, preserve and promote one's life. It also implies a proper regard for the human body itself and a duty not to willingly accept or deliberately inflict on oneself any physical mutilation that is not necessary for the good of the whole organism (Childless J, 1986 : 353)

Religion on life
In African societies life-force is the meaning of being and the ultimate goal of anyone is to acquire life and live happily. Everyone strives to enhance life and to be protected from misfortune or from a diminution of life or of being (Tempels P, 1959: 44-45). Supreme happiness is to possess the greatest life-force and the worst misfortune is the diminution of this force which is brought about by illness, sorcery and witchcraft or other evil forces. Life-force is granted by God, promoted by ancestors and enhanced by mystical power that is possessed by some people such as medicine men. Whatever or whoever increases the life force is good and whatever or whoever decreases or destroys it is bad.

A person is good in so far as he or she promotes, supports or protects his or her life force and the life-force of his or her neighbours. Alternatively, a person is bad or evil in as much as he or she undermines or destroys this life-force. The quest for life and its enhancement is the most fundamental value in African religions which governs all the other values.

Similarly, according to the Christian teaching, life is sacred because it was created by God. It is given to a person by God not in absolute ownership, but as a treasure to be administered and for which each person will have to account to God (Mt. 25: 14-30; Lk. 19: 12-27). Everyone has a duty to respect his or her own life and the life of others. Thus, Christianity emphasises the 'sanctity of life' as embodied in the fifth commandment "Thou shalt not kill". Killing in this context means taking away the life of an innocent person including oneself.

In Islam, life is sacred and must be preserved and protected. Islam teaches that aggression against human life is the second greatest sin in the sight of Allah, second only to denial of Him. Thus, anything which takes away innocent life or leads to loss of human life is condemned and prohibited to Muslims.

The Baha'i Faith, like Christianity and Islam, regards human life as sacred which should be preserved and protected. Violence is strongly condemned.

It should be noted that there are two dimensions in life and death issues; namely, the preservation and promotion of one's life and respect of other people's lives. The moral debate on the promotion and preservation of one's life centres on respect for both life and physical integrity. This brings to light issues related to individual habits which promote or threaten life. The African respect for life cannot be overemphasised in the face of the rising rates of suicide and the prevalence of life threatening habits such as drug abuse and alcoholism.

Drug abuse
Although it may not be on the same scale as in Europe, drug abuse in Africa has increased and has become an issue of moral concern. Drug abuse occurs when a drug is acquired illegally and is continually or sporadically used to excess, for reasons other than those for which it was manufactured and distributed (Searle C, 1984: 495). The World Health Organisation 'Expert Committee on Addiction Producing Drugs' recognises three distinct categories of drug abuse namely drug habituation, drug addiction and drug dependence.

Drug habituation is a form of drug abuse where the person concerned resorts to drug-taking in order to satisfy a psychological need only but he or she experiences no malaise when supplies are withdrawn from him or her. Drug addiction is a form of drug abuse wherein the person concerned resorts to drug-taking in order to satisfy both a psychological and a physiological need, and he or she experiences symptoms of malaise when supplies are withdrawn. On the other hand, drug dependence is a form of drug abuse where the person concerned resorts to drug-taking in order to satisfy a physiological need only, and wherein he or she experiences symptoms of malaise when supplies of a particular drug are withdrawn.

The effects of drug abuse on a person's health, economic welfare and social relations, have certain moral implications. Drug abuse causes personality deterioration, erratic changes in behaviour, emotional disturbance, physical problems such as bronchitis and asthma. It may also cause genetic damage, and mental problems such as schizophrenia and hypomania. Often a drug abuser's job suffers and may be lost, the family is tormented as it tries to save him or her, and society is affected since an abuser often takes to crime. As one becomes more dependent on drugs one needs more money to buy them which he or she may steal if he or she does not have it. Often drug abusers end by committing suicide.

Even casual use of drugs may pose moral problems. Some intoxicants deprive the person of judgement and self-respect. The wrongness lies in the fact that to deprive oneself of free consciousness, even with no risk of wrong doing, is an abdication of human responsibility. Even to reduce free-consciousness, say by use of tranquillisers, unless for a good purpose should be guarded against, especially because of its long term effects. The effects of the abuse of drugs on others, other than the one taking them, is also relevant in moral consideration.

Whereas drugs existed in African societies, there is no evidence that they were ever abused to an alarming degree. Their use was never of social concern. Consequently, African religions are silent about the moral implications of drug abuse and its related problems.

The general Christian position on drug abuse is to condemn it on the grounds that it impairs the function of one's brain. The Christian teaching is that one's body is the temple of God which should not be desecrated. Drug abuse is regarded as one of the sins which defile the body. If drugs are taken for the sole purpose of altering one's state of mind, the action is condemnable because it interferes with God's arrangement for a person. Some Christian groups discourage drug use on the grounds that the effects the drugs evoke in a person are, according to the New Testament, the exclusive work of the Holy Spirit in the personality of each Christian.

According to Islam, any substance which befogs the mind, impairing its faculties of thought, perception and discernment is prohibited. Therefore, use let alone abuse of drugs such as marijuana, cocaine and opium is prohibited. Islam prohibits use of such drugs mainly because they affect the sensory perception and impair reasoning and decision making. Such drugs make a person escape from the inner reality of one's feelings and the outer realities of life. In addition, drugs are prohibited because of their physical effects on a person such as bodily lassitude, dullness of their nerves, and decline in overall health. Perhaps the worst effects of drugs, according to Islam, is moral insensitivity, the weakening of the will power and neglect of responsibilities. Addiction which may result makes a person a diseased member of the community and may result in the destruction of family or even in a life of crime.

In addition, Islam recognises that obtaining drugs is very expensive and that this makes a drug abuser deprive his or her family the necessities of life in order to purchase drugs. She or he may resort to illegal means to pay for them.

The Baha'i Faith prohibits use of all mind-altering drugs such as opium, hahish, dagga, marijuana, cocaine, glue sniffing or any other drug in this category. Drugs are prohibited because they affect the mind and the body and cause people to act unwisely and irresponsibly.

Drug abuse is increasingly becoming a great danger to African societies and cannot be ignored any longer. One possible step to take against drug abuse is for the governments to control or ban completely, from public access, those drugs which are harmful and to empower the doctors to regulate their use. Tolerable drugs such as nicotine, mild tranquillizers and narcotics, which cannot be banned because of their social functions, could be put under general control for example, by limitation of access. In doing so, however, great care should be taken to ensure that banning and controls are not counter-productive.

There are other problems which are involved in drug control. Firstly, the line between use and abuse is not always clear. Many patients who use drugs as medicine may develop a dependence by which they demand increasing doses and show withdrawal symptoms when they stop using those drugs. There are also beverages which on the whole have a good effect but in some cases can cause ill-health and addiction. The common ones are tea and coffee with caffeine, cocoa with bromine and cola with caffeine. Although some religious groups such as Mormons abstain from them and prohibit their use, it becomes difficult for a government to decide on which drugs to ban or control and which ones to legalise. Secondly, what would be used to excess and, therefore, harmful in one place may not be in another. This, too, makes control difficult.

Another possible step is for governments to introduce penal laws for drug abuse. Penal laws, however, should be directed to drug dealers and not the abusers who, in their addicted state, are rather ill and suffering people who deserve help rather than punishment. Heavy taxes and restrictions to access can help to reduce addiction and abuse but may not work alone. Public information and education is perhaps of greater value than efforts to ban and control drugs. Accordingly, more emphasis should be put on education than on legal sanctions and restrictions.

Since the youth are the most venerable group, they deserve special attention in any endeavours to educate the public about the dangers of drug abuse. The family, as it has always been the case in Africa, is the starting place for this type of education.

Smoking

The morality of smoking has two dimensions. One is the issue of self-preservation and respect for one's life which relates to the smoker and his or her life. The other is the issue of social responsibility which concerns the smoker and the society in general.

Smoking is linked to greater probability of disease, disability, loss of productivity and an impaired quality of life. All these hazards have ethical implications since they affect the quality of life of the smoker and the community in which he or she lives.

Smoking is a common practice in African societies. Among the Batoro of Uganda, for example, when an important visitor arrives, he or she is given a pipe to smoke, coffee berries to chew as well as food and drink. In many African societies, "The lit pipe symbolizes acceptability; it is a token of sharing something together - breathing in unity the breath of life" (Mbiti J. 1969:138). Although it is acceptable, smoking in big gatherings is prohibited because it inconveniences non-smokers. In some societies. Such as the Banyankore of Uganda, children are not allowed to smoke and smoking etiquette does not permit women to smoke in public.

There is no common position on smoking on which all Christian churches agree. Some denominations are silent about the practice while others are not. A good example is the Seventh-day Adventist church which prohibits smoking and is totally opposed to it. According to this church, there is a distinct relationship between one's religion and one's physical and social habits such as smoking. Seventh-day Adventists believe that though composed of different parts, a person is a unit and that various parts of an individual interact with each other, and what affects one will affect the others. Since smoking affects the body it is believed to affect the soul. Before a person is baptised into the Seventh-day Adventist church he or she must give an assurance not to smoke and the course of instruction to candidates includes practical lessons on how to quit smoking.

Although the Seventh Day Adventist church may be the only one explicitly opposed to smoking, some churches would regard smoking as an act of uncleanliness (Gal. 5:19) and against the gospel of holiness (Mat. 5:48). Most churches, however, treat smoking indifferently and leave individuals to decide whether to smoke or not.

In Islam smoking is *Makruh*. Although it is not specifically prohibited like drugs and alcohol, smoking is discouraged. The general principle is that a Muslim should not take anything which may cause his or her death, either quickly or gradually. Any substance which is injurious to health or harmful to the body is prohibited. Smoking is discouraged on the grounds that it is harmful to health and that it is narcotic, the use of which is forbidden by Islamic law. Smoking is also discouraged because smoke irritates those who do not practise the habit and because it is economically wasteful with no tangible benefits. The issue becomes even more serious when the money spent on smoking is otherwise needed for the sustenance of oneself or one's family.

The position of the Baha'i Faith on smoking is not clear. While the teaching of the Faith strongly discourages its use, it does not forbid it. The Guardian of the Faith said that no one has a right to prevent anyone from smoking and that the Baha'is are free to smoke, but it was preferable for them not to do so. On the other hand, Abdu'l Baha' condemned smoking in the strongest terms:

> I wish to say that, in the sight of God, the smoking of tobacco is a thing which is blamed and condemned, very unclean, and of which the result is by degrees injurious. Besides it is a cause of expense and of loss of time and it is a harmful habit.... (Abdu'l Baha', : 335).

In short, smoking, though not prohibited in the Baha'i Faith, is discouraged.

Religion apart, individual smokers have a duty to promote their well-being which requires avoiding any act that is contrary to that duty. More especially, smokers should consider the effects of smoking on others. It has been established that smoking has negative effects even those people who do not smoke, but who live or work in close proximity of smokers. This is known as involuntary smoking which is a cause of lung cancer in non-smokers. In addition, bronchitis, laryngitis, pneumonia and other respiratory infections are more common in children whose parents smoke, compared with the children of non-smokers. It has also been discovered that unborn babies whose mothers smoke are unfortunately passive smokers. At birth they are smaller in size and weigh less than babies whose mothers do not smoke. They are also likely to be stillborn, or to die in the first few weeks of life. It should also be noted that non-smokers in smoky rooms often experience discomfort. In short, passive and involuntary smoking caused by smokers violates the right to health of non-smokers and should as much as possible be avoided. The African social etiquette should bind smokers not to smoke in public places.

Alcoholism

Alcoholism is a serious health and social problem in Africa, raising concern in various circles in society. Alcoholism means addiction to alcohol and loss of control over one's drinking habits. It is a mental and physical illness with complex social and psychological dimensions which originate from excessive and continuous consumption of alcohol.

Alcoholism is a stage of drinking when a person cannot control his drinking habits and almost every drinking leads to drunkenness. If a person drinks heavily, constantly, his or her body develops tolerance and drinks more amounts to get the same effect. Because of this, there is a gradual physical and mental deterioration of the drinker. This becomes progressively worse and the alcoholic is driven further and further from normal life. This may end in chronic alcoholism which is the most severe form of alcoholism when a person has a compulsion to drink continually (Searle C, 1984:508).

Not all forms of alcoholic consumption, however, are alcoholism. Alcohol, for example, is sometimes administered and consumed as medicine. Alcohol in various forms is also often served and consumed moderately at social functions. These forms of drinking are not harmful to health or society. In fact, it is perhaps correct to say that the majority of adults in African societies take alcoholic beverages without becoming alcoholics. In moral discourse, therefore, it is important to put a distinction between moderate social and excessive drinking.

Social drinking is a form of drinking in which a person occasionally drinks with friends in order to be sociable. It is usually moderate and the drinker does not drink himself or herself to drunkenness. Sometimes, however, social drinking exceeds normal expectations resulting in excessive drinking. The drinker gets drunk leading to the complications which accompany heavy drinking such as hangover, accidents and sickness. This form of drinking may lead to alcoholism.

There are many dangers to one's life and to society arising from excessive drinking and alcoholism. One of these is loss of proper control of oneself which leads to doing things one would not do in his or her sober mood. In such a state one does things which lead to loss of self and other people's respect. One's morals and other values are blunted by alcohol and fights or promiscuity may follow. This may lead to a sense of guilt and regret the following day.

Many crimes, too, are committed under the influence of alcohol. There are also unpleasant effects of alcoholism on health. Diseases such as the cirrhosis of the liver, pancreatitis and alcohol hepatitis are caused by excessive use of alcohol, so are chronic gastritis and diseases which are caused by underfeeding and malnutrition such as beriberi and pellagra. Many drinkers sustain bruises and fractures through accidents resulting from acting under the influence of alcohol.

Excessive alcohol taken with or without other drugs may, and has many times, caused death. In addition, accidental death, either at home, on the road or at the place of work, may be caused by excessive consumption of alcohol. Even when death is not immediate, excessive consumption of alcohol may lead to the deterioration of bodily functions and organs such as the brain and the heart. Eventually this may lead to death.

Excessive drinking is also associated with social problems. The immediate group which feels the pinch of an alcoholic is the family. For married people, it may lead to fights at home and to child abuse. Many cases of separation and divorce are caused by excessive drinking. There are also people who lose their jobs or whose studies are interrupted because alcohol has interfered with their brains and affected their ability to make proper judgement in different situations.

These are just a few of the undesirable consequences of excessive consumption of alcohol. Alcoholism is certainly an individual and social problem that calls for serious individual and social attention.

African religions accept alcohol consumption and alcohol plays a very important part in religious life. On almost every important occasion beer or wine is served; ceremonies, festivities, marriage negotiations, land contracts, wedding parties, or social visits, are all occasions for drinking. Alcohol is a symbol of friendship, communion, oneness and acceptability in the community.

From time to time wine or beer is used to pour libation for the ancestors or to give them a drink. On those occasions when wine or beer is served to ancestors, it is left in the shrine overnight and the following day the family drinks what the ancestors have 'left over'.

Although alcohol consumption is accepted and alcohol is served on many functions, drunkenness is discouraged and condemned. A person is expected to drink moderately and at the right time with the right type of people.

There is no single position held by all Christian churches as far as alcohol consumption is concerned. Whereas some churches tolerate moderate drinking, many others prohibit their members from drinking even small amounts. Several reasons are given for this position but a more profound motive seems to be that alcohol substitutes a false physical euphoria for one based on spiritual freedom and strength, and on the Holy Spirit (Eph. 5:18).

The general spirit of the Old Testament tolerates moderate drinking but condemns drunkenness. Excessive eating and drinking are condemned together (Prov. 23:20). In the Old Testament times consumption of alcohol, in a form of wine, was common and normal. Wine and milk were the most common beverages. There were times, however, when wine was forbidden. The use of wine or any other fermented drink, for example, was forbidden to the priests during all the time they were in the tabernacle and employed in the service of the altar (Lev. 10:9). Alcoholic drinks were also forbidden to Nazarites. Otherwise, wine and corn denoted all sorts of good things (Genesis 27: 28-37)

In the New Testament, too, moderate drinking is accepted and even encouraged. Jesus himself drank wine and produced it for a wedding feast (Jn

2:1-11). Paul also recommends it to Timothy for the comfort of his stomach (1 Tim. 5:23). At the same time drunkenness is condemned (Lk. 21:34, Rom. 13:13, Gal. 5:21.

Whereas some churches such as the Nazarene, Free Evangelical, Seventh Day Adventist and Assemblies of God totally prohibit use of alcohol, others such as the Anglican, Roman Catholic and Methodist churches tolerate moderate use. However, they all condemn drunkenness.

Islam prohibits the use of all sorts of intoxicants, no matter what amount. Consumption of even small amounts is prohibited. The Quran is uncompromisingly against taking alcohol (5:94). It is not only those who consume intoxicants that are condemned. Prophet Muhammad is reported to have said that ten types of people, in connection with intoxicants, have been cursed by Allah:

> The one who squeezes it and he who has it squeezed; He who drinks it and he who gives it to another to drink; he who carries it to somebody, he who has it brought to him; he who sells it; he who purchases it; he who presents it as a gift and finally he who brings to use proceeds there from.

Islam forbids use of alcohol because it destroys physical and mental health.

Similarly, alcohol consumption is prohibited by the Baha'i Faith. No Baha'i is allowed to take alcohol no matter what quantity except when it is prescribed by a doctor. When a doctor has no alternative treatment, he may use alcohol and in that case a patient takes it as medicine. This applies to drugs and intoxicating herbs as well.

As already noted above, in African societies alcohol consumption has always been associated with all important religious, social, or political occasions. However, because it was consumed according to sanctioned ways which regulated and moderated drinking, alcohol did not create serious individual or social problems. However, the problem of alcoholism has arisen as a result of social changes which have overtime changed drinking patterns. A comparison of some features of the traditional and modern drinking patterns shows that whereas alcoholic consumption in traditional societies was moderate and manageable and create few serious problems, it is only in modern societies that alcoholism has become a matter of grave moral concern.

The nature of traditional alcoholic drinks could not cause serious problems because alcoholic beverages were made from fermented cereals or fruits such as millet, maize, sorghum, bananas and several others. The products of these cereals or fruits had a high nutritional value in terms of vitamins, carbohydrates and proteins. Consequently, traditional brews were not a serious threat to health. Most of the drinks which were introduced in Africa, and are sold in bars and bottle stores have a high alcoholic content that leads to drunkenness, poor health and social irresponsibility.

It is not only the nature of drinks that has changed but also the mode of drinking. Traditionally, there were limits in the usage of alcoholic beverages; drinking was regulated according to age, sex, and time. Alcohol consumption, for example, was limited to adults. Most occasions and functions during which alcohol was served were attended only by adults. Only on special occasions, especially religious ones, were children allowed to taste it. These days alcoholic drinks are sold in bars, bottle stores and *sheebeens* from where even boys and girls can buy some to drink.

Another important drinking pattern which has changed is the company during drinking. Traditionally, men and women drank separately. These days men mix with women in bars and other drinking places. The result is that men often fight over women and sometimes cases of rape and other forms of sexual immorality are reported.

It has been noted that traditionally, drinking was an expression of fellowship to cement social relationships. It was an activity which brought friends and relatives together. As a result, there was mutual concern. In that context, drinking was supervised and moderation was emphasised. In bars and hotels people drink with strangers who are not concerned about their reputation or well-being. A person is only limited in his or her drinking by money; a phenomenon that leads to drunkenness and related problems such as road accidents.

Drunkenness was also reduced by restricting time for drinking. Drinking started late in the afternoon or in the evening, when work had been done and people had had lunch, and people returned to their homes early after such social drinking session. The situation has been changed by the commercialisation of alcohol. Some bars are open during working hours and night clubs sell alcohol throughout the night, until morning.

Another negative result of commercialising alcoholic consumption is that some people spend most of their earnings on drinking and neglect their parental or marital financial duties. This is a situation that could not have arisen in a traditional setting because drinking was an occasion for fellowship and alcoholic drinks were served free of charge.

So whereas alcohol consumption is always associated with moral problems of varying degrees, the use of alcohol in traditional societies was not as destructive to individuals or to society as it is today. There has been a change in the drinking patterns which has resulted in the deterioration of moral standards in terms of who should drink when, what, where and with whom. As much as possible, the African drinking culture should be revived.

Suicide

Another serious moral issue in matters of life and death is suicide which is the voluntary causing of one's own death or intentionally killing oneself. It involves taking one's own life, knowingly and willingly, usually from one's own hand or personally arranging the conditions for the termination of one's life.

There are three basic positions concerning suicide. The first is that one's life is personal and, therefore, one has a right to terminate it, if he or she so wishes. Some people who hold this view would even go as far as advocating it as an honourable act of bravery. The second view is that suicide is immoral and sinful and that it is never justifiable for any reason. A third, and moderate, position is that suicide is evil but may be resorted to as a necessary evil in some situations such as in the event of an incurable and painful disease or in order to escape torture.

There is a distinction between taking one's life, and giving it; between a person who intentionally seeks death for its own sake as a benefit for himself or herself and another who seeks it in order to benefit others or for the sake of a higher cause. This is a distinction between a self-regarding and an other-regarding suicide.

A person may justifiably offer his or her life or put it in serious danger for a higher cause such as God's glory, the salvation of souls or the service of one's friends or relatives. This is sacrificial death. Whereas in suicide a person desires death for its own sake, in sacrificial death a person has greater intentions which are not selfish or cowardly; the welfare of others or a noble cause. In this category one includes martyrs who are prepared to die for their faith or nation, performing a duty in war, defending a friend or relative who is unjustly attacked, and nursing the infectious sick. In each of these cases a person does not will his or her death but is prepared to accept it as an unavoidable consequence of an act of duty, charity, justice, mercy or pity. A person in such cases dies for a cause greater than himself or herself. However, not all people would agree with this reasoning. They would say that the ultimate loyalty of a person is to himself or herself.

There is also a difference between killing oneself and refusing to save oneself. A person in great pain may shoot himself, causing his own death. This is active suicide. On the other hand, a patient in the hospital may refuse treatment which would have prolonged his or her life, thus leading to his or her own death. The latter form of suicide is a passive one. It is at times argued that refusing to act is in itself action and therefore passive suicide is as bad as active suicide. Perhaps the major consideration here is the intention and knowledge that the act will lead to one's death.

Suicide in African religions is regarded both as immoral, sinful and condemned on both moral and religious grounds. It is, for example, believed that a person who commits suicide does not become an ancestor. The belief is that after one's death, a person travels to the land of the ancestors where he or she rejoins the dead members of the family. After death, therefore, a number of rituals are performed to help the departed's soul to travel and arrive safely in the land of ancestors. These rituals are not performed for a person who commits suicide because it is believed that such a person cannot become an ancestor. He or she is believed to become a ghost which may become a nuisance to the family and the whole clan.

It should be noted, however, that it is honourable in African societies for a person to risk one's life for the sake of others. A person who dies at war or while defending a friend or relative from an animal or an enemy is glorified by the community. Surrendering one's life for the greater life of the community is not regarded as immoral. It is even praised.

The Christian teaching is that because a person is not the absolute owner of his or her life, it is not for him or her to decide for how long it shall be used. Suicide, therefore, is regarded as a sin against God, a rejection of his love and a denial of his sovereignty; an offence against the proper love of one's own person; a violation of the fifth commandment and an act of despair which precludes redemption. Suicide is also regarded as an offence against mankind in that it both deprives society in general and one's own family of a member prematurely and also denies them an opportunity of ministering to his or her needs (Childress J, 1986: 609).

According to Islam, a person is not entirely his or her own master; he or she was created by, and belongs, to Allah. Whoever takes his or her life by any means whatsoever, has unjustly taken a life which Allah has made sacred. So one is not allowed to diminish it, let alone to harm or destroy it (Al-Qaradawi Y, 1985: 327). In addition, a person is an asset to his or her religion and community. Thus, his or her life, health, wealth and all that Allah has bestowed upon him or her are a trust which he or she is not permitted to diminish. The Quran clearly prohibits killing oneself (4:29) or doing anything that may ruin one's life (2:195).

While recognising that the world is full of woes and suffering, the Baha'i Faith advocates bravery and a stout heart while in it. Trials and tribulations should arouse added rigour and greater determination in a person rather than dampen his or her zeal to endure them. In the Baha'i Faith, suicide is forbidden on the grounds that God, who is the author of all life, alone can take it away and dispose of it in the way he deems best. The teaching is that a person who commits suicide endangers his or her soul, and will, as a result, suffer spiritually in the other worlds beyond (Hornby H, 1988: 203).

Debate surrounds suicide as a moral issue. Some people doubt whether suicide is a moral issue arguing that morality is concerned with relations with other people and to them suicide is a personal act. If one argues this way, one is inclined to say that suicide is a purely individual act that one may or may not do. This view, however, seems to disregard the effect of suicide on other people. A person is a social animal with social obligations. Committing suicide deprives the society one of its members and of the services one would have rendered to the community.

The act of suicide has the greatest impact on the family especially in cases where the person has a spouse and children. Members of the family are deprived of his or her love, presence and company. They are also deprived of the services required of him or her. It means, therefore, that suicide is not a purely personal matter; it is an act with social implications and, therefore, a moral issue.

Another argument in favour of suicide is based on the principle of individual autonomy or self-rule, namely that, over one's own body and mind, the individual is sovereign and has the right and freedom to kill oneself. The argument is that on this principle of liberty, the freedom to do what one desires, no one should interfere with another person's freedom if the exercise of that freedom does not interfere with the rights of others, especially if such a person is an adult, rational and free.

The argument against this reasoning is that life is so valuable that no one may throw it away as he or she chooses. In fact, it may be argued that suicide is the only act which a person is not free to do or not to do. As Crawford contends, suicide is the ultimate challenge to a person's freedom, for it will end his freedom (Crawford, 1991:14). It is a decision to end one's freedom which puts the person out of any freedom to act.

Several factors need to be taken into consideration when discussing the morality or immorality of suicide. Of particular importance are the motives and the consequences of the act. These ought to be kept at the forefront in the suicide debate. It is also important to distinguish between a coldly premeditated and an utterly compulsive suicide. In other words, in any particular case, the degree of culpability depends upon the state of mind and the social or environmental circumstances in which suicide is done. This is because, more often than not, people understand that suicide is not voluntary and therefore not blameworthy. Usually a person who commits suicide is under strong emotional stress or physical pain. Under such circumstances, it is difficult to say that a person is wholly acting voluntarily. The difficult state of the mind certainly diminishes moral responsibility for the act.

Since suicide is, to some degree, socially 'contagious', once a family member or any other person in the community commits suicide, an effort should be made to prevent its recurrence. A major cause of suicide is isolation, loneliness, and lack of communal support and understanding. Suicide in African societies was rare because of the care and mutuality which characterised these societies. Thus, it is a challenge to every African to maintain or rediscover mutuality and as much as possible to live according to African values of communal solidarity as much as is possible.

Chapter Five

RESPECT FOR OTHER PEOPLE'S LIVES

It is generally agreed that life is so priceless that we should respect other people's lives and that one should not use violence against another person without good reasons. Yet social violence in the form of institutionalised violence by police and army, revolutionary violence by liberation groups and international violence in the form of war are very common in Africa. So is violence between individuals involving assault and homicide, especially in the case of gangs and criminals.

Culpable homicide
Homicide refers to the taking of another person's life. Not all forms of homicide, however, are morally blameworthy. Killing another person accidentally, for example, is not morally blameworthy. Nor is justifiable homicide such as killing during the war. The form of homicide considered in this chapter is culpable homicide when a person kills another intentionally without acceptable reasons.

As already noted, in African societies, life-force is a central value. Whatever increases it is good, and whatever decreases it is bad. Wrong is anything that destroys or harms one's life-force or the life-force of others (Tempels P, 1959:45). Following from that reasoning, life is intrinsically valuable and it is everyone's duty to support and nourish one's life and those of others, especially of one's relatives. To kill an innocent person, unless it is done for acceptable reasons, is not permitted. The acceptable reasons would include self-defence and the administration of justice.

In African societies, because of the corporate nature of existence, if a member of the family or clan murders a person, the whole group shares in his or her guilt. The dead person's family or clan may take the life of the murderer or of any member of his or her family or clan in the cause of justice.

According to Christianity, a person's right to life, which is grounded in divine origin, is the basis of all human rights, natural and legal, and the foundation of civilised society (Childress J, 1986: 253). The commandment "Thou shalt not kill" is based on this principle. Everyone has a duty to cherish, protect and preserve human life of every other person from conception to death. This implies a secondary duty for taking all moral means for the relief of suffering and the eradication of disease and prevention of death, if possible, of other people.

On these grounds and because of the belief that God is the absolute owner of human beings, it is regarded as immoral and sinful to deliberately assault or kill an innocent person.

Homicide is prohibited and condemned in Islam. According to Islam, Allah created human life and made it sacred and it belongs to him. The Quran clearly prohibits the taking of human life without a just cause (17:33).

Qias is a principle in Islam of life for life and if a person kills another without a good reason, justice on the grounds of *qias* is administered. This is done according to guidelines given by the Quran:

> O ye who believe!
> The law of equality
> Is prescribed to you
> In cases of murder:
> The free for the free
> The slave for the slave
> The woman for the woman
> (11:178)

Thus, Islam accepts justice of life for life, but puts distinction between the life of a free person and the life of a slave, and between the life of a man and the life of a woman. Murder is prohibited and 'life for life' is meant to discourage it.

In the Baha'i Faith, peace and mutual co-existence are key values whose essence is to attain the unity of mankind. As a result, the Faith condemns all forms of violence including vengeance because no good result is gained by the avenger and because it is returning evil for evil. It is argued that returning a blow for a blow, for example, cannot be a balm for the wound or a remedy for the pain. Both, the first and the second blow, are regarded as injuries, the difference being that one occurred first and the other afterward. The Faith advocates forgiveness and mercy and censures revenge. A Baha'i is required to return good for evil. One should not only forgive the aggressor or oppressor but if possible one should be of service to him or her. So homicide even in a form of revenge is forbidden (Abdul Baha, 1981: 269).

Most people will agree that a person's right to life is conferred upon him or her by God - not by other people. It is his or hers by virtue of being human. Therefore, it is not within the moral competence of any individual deliberately to attack or destroy it. Thus, in most cases, it is never permissible to make any deliberate attack upon the life of another person, even at the other's invitation.

However, a person may be killed by accident; as a result of actions that have been in no sense willed either by the dead person or by any other person. In this case, neither the dead person nor the others involved are morally to blame. It is when a person freely assaults or kills another person that he or she is morally to blame.

The general principle is that an individual should not resort to the use of force to advance one's interests, not even to assert his or her rights or to defend them, because public authority is there to do so. The popular cliche' is that people should not "take the law into their hands". Consequently, violence, the exercise of physical force to inflict injury on, or cause damage to, a person or property is evil. However, there are situations which justify resort to violence as a necessary evil. Violence in self-defence is one such a case.

Self-defence
Although some people would say that under no circumstances is anyone justified to use violence or even to kill another, there are others who would say that at times there are situations when the use of violence, even homicide, is morally justified. The latter group argue that the right to life implies the right to protect and defend it against an aggressor. It is also argued that a person has an obligation to protect the life of another person, especially a friend or relative, against an attacker. On these grounds, it is argued that one may be justified to use violence in defence of one's children, parents, wife, husband or neighbour.

Yet self-defence can be effective only if it is in proportion to the violence of the aggressor. This means that in the process of self-defence one may kill the attacker. In addition it is argued that violence, including homicide, can be used to defend goods which are equivalent to life. These are goods without which life is not 'worth living'. These would include wealth, liberty, sanity, chastity and, at times, bodily completeness. In defence of one's virginity, for example, a girl may rightly kill a rapist, if that is the only way she can stop him and defend her wholesomeness.

Whereas some people would justify assault or homicide, in defence of one's honour or reputation as a way to silence the slanderer, there are others who do not. They argue that since one's honour and reputation can only be defended by truth, it is not morally justifiable to assault or kill a slanderer. Violence, in this case, would only prove physical strength, but would not restore one's honour or reputation.

Defence of goods, some people would say, extends to material goods and would justify killing a robber, if that is the only way to stop him. Others would not accept this position and argue that material goods can never be as valuable as the life of a person, a robber in this case.

In African ethical thinking, violence in self-defence is justifiable. A person has a duty to defend his or her life against attack. Consequently, a person may hurt or even kill another person if that is the only option he or she has.

In Africa, existence is understood in terms of the group and an individual exists corporately. Self-defence, therefore, extends to one's friends, relatives, and other members of the community. If anyone of them is attacked, every other person has a duty to defend him or her. Consequently, a person may assault or even kill in order to defend one's friend, relative or neighbour.

Christians are not agreed on the issue of self-defence. On the one hand, there are some Christians and churches who accept it as a necessary evil, as much as a just war is accepted. Their view is that some violations of God's law may occur within the framework of God's love. For example, many Christian groups will agree that a person is morally justified to steal in order to feed a starving person or to tell a lie in order to save an innocent person from murder. They also argue that acts which would otherwise be wrong are rendered rightful by a good purpose or by the necessity of choosing a lesser evil (Lk. 22:35-36). Thus, resorting to violence, even if it means killing, in self-defence may become a necessary evil and morally justifiable.

Other Christian groups, especially the evangelical ones, reject this view and condemn self-defence on scriptural grounds. They argue that Jesus repudiated any right to self-defence both through his teaching and examples (Jn. 18:10; Mt. 5: 38-42; Lk. 6:29,30). According to them, even under extreme pressure the Christian does not assert the claims of self-interest, instead he or she meets violence with love (Rom. 12:17-21; 1 Cor. 13:4-7; 1 Thes. 5:15). These churches teach non resistance to aggression (1 Pet. 2:23), whether individual or institutional.

Islam allows a person to fight or kill in self defence. This is based on the Quran:

> To those against whom
> War is made, permission
> Is given (to fight) because
> They are wronged; -and verily,
> God is Most Powerful
> For their aid;-
> (22:39)

Although the Baha'i Faith condemns violence, it permits people to defend themselves when attacked by an aggressor. Abdul Baha taught, for example, that in case of attack by robbers or gangsters a Baha'i should not surrender himself, but should try, as far as circumstances permit, to defend himself, and later on lodge a complaint with the government authorities. In an emergency, when there is no legal force at hand to appeal to, a Baha'i is justified in defending his or her life. The Baha'i, however, should not go beyond self-defence into retaliation, which is forbidden by the Faith. A person is required to be guided by conscience to decide when to stop in the process of self-defence (Hornby

H, 1988: 116-117). However, when attacked as a Baha'i, on religious grounds, one is not permitted to defend himself with violence. Religious persecution is not a valid reason for self-defence.

Whereas it is acceptable, and indeed a duty, for a person to defend himself or herself, certain conditions must be fulfilled to justify assault or homicide in self-defence. One of them is the motive. The motive to assault or to kill must be self-defence, not hatred, revenge or any other evil intention. Secondly, the violence used against the attacker must be applied only at the time of attack, not before, or after. The threat of attack or fear of it, for example, do not justify violence in self-defence. Thirdly, violence should be used only when there is no other way of repelling attack. If one can call the police, dissuade the attacker from his or her action, run away or do something else to protect himself or herself, one should not resort to violence in self-defence. Fourthly, in self-defence no more violence or injury than necessary may be used or afflicted to event the danger. The injury inflicted should be within the limits of a blameless defence.

What has been said about self-defence against an unjust aggressor also applies to an innocent aggressor such as the mentally disturbed or one who does not realise that what he or she is doing may kill someone. Since self-defence is not a way of punishing the aggressor but self-preservation, one is still morally justified to harm or kill an innocent aggressor in order to protect oneself.

It should be emphasised that in self-defence, the aim is not to kill or even to harm the aggressor, but to produce a state of non-activity in him or her so that he or she cannot continue the attack. Killing an aggressor, for example when cutting off his arm would stop his or her aggression, justifiable as an act of self-defence. This does not mean that killing the aggressor must always be avoided. In self-defence a person may aim at killing the aggressor, if it is necessary.

Abortion
Presently, many African societies are experiencing a high rate of premarital pregnancies among the youth, especially among school children. Because of the social stigma, school policies and negative attitudes associated with out of wedlock pregnancy which interfere with the happiness and future of a pregnant single girl, increasingly girls who get pregnant before marriage choose to abort.

Abortion is not practised by single women only. Both single and married women in Africa are caught between the challenges of modern living and traditional values which emphasise respect for human life, big families and community. Because of modern conditions which militate against having big families, the inconvenience of having a child at a given time, say during examinations, economic hardships, divorce, separation or any other reason which leads to an extra child being unwelcome, some married women, too, resort to abortion.

Abortion as a moral issue refers to the deliberate termination of a pregnancy before the foetus is capable of surviving outside the womb. Foetus in this book refers to the unborn being, at whatever stage of development, during the nine months of pregnancy.

Abortion is a serious moral issue with wide-ranging implications for the foetus itself, the mother, the father and the community at large. In considering the morality of abortion, therefore, one should take into consideration all the parties involved.

As a social phenomenon, abortion has been resorted to for a variety of reasons and by a variety of methods. Similarly, there has always been a variety of opinions regarding the morality of it. Currently, opinions about abortion still vary, ranging from utter condemnation to free choice. The basic issue has been "Up to what point of foetal development, if any, and for what reasons, if any, is abortion morally acceptable?" One extreme view is that abortion is never morally acceptable, or at least it is acceptable only when it is necessary to save the life of the mother. The opposite extreme view is that abortion is always morally acceptable, at any point of foetal development and for any of the 'standard' reasons (Mappes T, 1982:2). In between these extreme positions, there is a diversity of moderate opinions which regard abortion as morally evil but tolerate some forms of it under certain circumstances or see it as morally acceptable only up to a certain point of foetal development.

The basic issues to be considered in this book are the status and rights of the unborn human life, the rights and welfare of the expectant mother and her self-determination of reproductive capacity, the rights and interests of the father, and the interests of the community as a whole (Childress J.F. 1986:1). All things being equal, each factor represents a value to be respected. The problem arises when all the above values cannot be given equal support or in which support of one precludes another. Disagreements about the morality of abortion arise from differing evaluations of the relative priority of these values in conflict cases.

A major point of contention in the abortion debate is the status and rights of an unborn human life. Anti-abortionists, popularly referred to as 'the conservatives' or "pro-life", claim that a foetus is a human being with full human moral rights, right from conception, and that abortion is consequently a form of homicide. On the other hand, the 'extreme liberals', who advocate free choice in abortion matters, believe that a foetus is on the same level with plants or animals and has no human status and rights and can be ejected from the womb whenever the mother chooses. The basic question, therefore, is the point of humanisation; when, in the development of a foetus, after fertilisation, humanisation takes place: "When does a foetus become human and therefore begin to have rights?"

Some people put humanisation at the point of fertilisation of the ovum. They argue that at this point the zygote is ready to develop into an individual human being, if nothing stops it. The argument being that the ovum, at this stage, is a genotype distinct from the mother and the father with a never-to-be repeated genetic code, which itself proceeds to further development. People who hold this view regard abortion, at any stage after fertilisation, except perhaps when the mother's life is in danger, as homicide and, therefore, morally objectionable (Mappes, T, 1982:3).

On the other hand, there are people who say that humanisation is associated with socialisation. People who hold this view put humanisation after birth. They contend that the foetus remains nonhuman even in the most advanced stages of development and because a foetus is not the same thing as a person, it is not attributed with moral status (Mappes T, 1982:3). In their view, killing a foetus before birth is not homicide.

The two positions above represent two extremes with moderate positions in between which may be briefly presented here. Some people put humanisation at the point of implantation into the womb, arguing, among other things, that humanity essentially includes a relationship to other people which is only clear at implantation. Yet others are of the view that the cortex is a necessary prerequisite for human life and put humanisation after the cerebral cortex has developed which is between the fifteenth and fortieth day, after fertilisation. There are even those who want to put the point of humanisation at quickening, when the foetus begins to move in the womb, and others at viability, when the foetus could continue to live outside the mother.

For each of these groups, before the time they regard as the point of humanisation, a foetus has no rights. Other things being equal, they would regard abortion only after the point of humanisation as homicide and therefore morally evil, but morally acceptable before that point. For many moderates, however, besides the point of humanisation in foetal development, the reasons why abortion is resorted to should be taken into consideration in judging whether a case of abortion is morally justifiable or not.

The other basic issue is the rights and welfare of the pregnant woman, including the right to self-determination of reproduction capacity. The question is: Does a woman have a right to decide whether or not to bear a child when she has already conceived it? One view, held by the pro-abortion group, is that a woman has this right and that access to abortion on demand is a necessary guarantee of reproductive self-determination. The pro-abortion view is that abortion must be available, at any time, to every woman at her own decision (Childress J.F, 1967: 3-4). According to this view, the foetus belongs to the mother and, others even contend that it is part of her body and, therefore, she can do with it what she wants. A contrary view is that the foetus, though in the woman's womb, belongs both to the mother and the father. Thus, the woman's rights are limited by the father's even when conception is out of wedlock.

Some people argue that the pregnancy does not belong to the mother alone, not even to the mother and the father only, but to the whole family and the whole community. The decision to terminate it, thus should not be an individual mother's but a corporate decision involving the parents and the community taking into consideration the seriousness of the need to commit it. The pro-abortion group does not accept this view.

According to African religions, killing a human being is a moral evil because it deprives the community of an additional member. Killing a person, young or old, is only acceptable if it is for the good of the community; either to strengthen or to save it. When a foetus threatens the life of the mother, for example, it may be aborted.

In African societies, the point of humanisation does not seem to cause a problem. The unborn human life, though still developing and has no independent existence, is a human being and not a thing or a part of the mother's body. In most African societies, as soon as the mother conceives, she reports the matter to the family and everyone is happy to know that a new member of the family is on the way. From that point, until long after birth, a number of rituals are performed and certain taboos and regulations are observed, not only because pregnancy places a woman in ritual state, but also to protect her and the prospective member of the family.

Most African societies are patriarchal and patrilineal. Authority in the home rests with the father and children trace their descent and kinship line through their father. That means that in those societies children belong primarily to the father. Similarly, the foetus does not belong to the mother alone but also to the father. In extreme cases, women are regarded as the fertile field in which a man sows his seeds and the 'crops' belong to the owner of the seeds and not the field itself. Although this view is changing, a child is still regarded, first and foremost, as the father's and only secondary the mother's. This means that a mother has limited rights on what she can do with a foetus. The view that the expectant mother owns the foetus and can do with it what she wants is not acceptable.

In addition, life is lived communally and an individual exists corporately. Individualism is something that has just been introduced by urbanisation,

Western education, the monetary economy and other foreign forces, but community spirit is still strong. The foetus, therefore, does not belong only to its parents but to the whole family and community.

The position on abortion varies among different churches. In all of them, however, the Christian doctrines of creation and redemption lead to positions in favour of preserving human life and enhancing its quality. Christian ethics of abortion centre on respect for the lives of all human individuals, the prohibition of the killing of innocent persons, and procreation as a potential outcome of sexual activity.

There is hardly any direct scriptural reference to abortion. In the Old Testament, abortion is mentioned indirectly. It is said, for example, that if men who are quarrelling cause a woman to miscarry, the guilty one shall pay a fine to the woman's husband, but if the woman herself be killed, then the attacker must "give life for life" (Ex. 21:22-23). This seems to suggest that whereas a woman is a full human being, a foetus is not full life to pay "life for life". However, a foetus is not regarded as sub-human or part of the mother. The Bible, for example, says, "For thou didst form my inward parts, thou didst knit me together in my mother's womb" (Ps. 139: 13-15). Thus, the Old Testament shows that God is involved in the formation of a person from conception (Gen. 4:1: Job 31:15: Isa. 44:24: 49:1; Jer. 1:5). In addition, the fifth commandment "You shall not kill" (Ex. 20:13) is interpreted as an unconditional prohibition of taking innocent human life from its beginnings in the womb, until the end God has set for it. In the New Testament, too, it is shown that God is involved in life in the womb (Mt. 1:18: Lk. 1:40, 42). The New Testament, however, does not make any specific reference to abortion.

Churches differ in their positions on abortion. The Catholic church, for example, condemns abortion at any stage, after fertilisation as a brutal, inhumane act involving the killing of an innocent human being. It teaches that from the time the ovum is fertilised, a life is began "which is neither that of the father nor of the mother", it is rather the life of a new human being with his or her own growth. The argument is that this ovum, after fertilisation, would never be made human if it were not human already.

The ruling of the church is that direct abortion of a child in the womb, for any reason whatsoever, even to preserve the life of the mother, is murder. Only an abortion in which the procedure is physically 'indirect' that is, one which does not destroy the foetus directly, being aimed at relieving the condition of the mother and resulting only secondarily in the death of the offspring, are allowed. Some of the examples given are the removal of a cancerous but pregnant uterus and excision of a fallopian tube in which exists an ectopic pregnancy. This is justified on the grounds of the *double effect principle*.

Among Protestant churches the status of the foetus is seen in relation to God's creation of the soul and predestination. However, procreation is no longer regarded as the sole, not even the primary, purpose of sexual activity. It is, among other things, seen to be directed equally to effective communication between sexual partners. Secondly, women have gained more and more moral and social autonomy and, as a result, claims are made in their favour of the right to decide whether or not to bear children, and to have access to abortion, as a necessary guarantee of reproductive self-determination. Thirdly, there is the controversy over the status of foetal life at the various stages of the pregnancy. Fourthly, there is the capacity to predict congenital abnormalities through genetic evaluation of parents or testing of the foetus *in utero* and aborting the offspring in whom abnormality is anticipated. As a result, most Protestant churches tolerate some forms of abortion. Many Protestant churches will, for example, tolerate abortion of a pregnancy which is a result of rape or which threatens the life of the mother.

Islam prohibits abortion and even doing violence to the pregnancy at any stage after it has occurred. The statement below summarises the Islamic position on abortion and clearly shows that it is a crime even to stop implantation, after fertilisation has taken place:

> Abortion is a crime against an existing being. Now, existence has stages. The first stages of existence are the settling of the semen in the womb and its mixing with the secretions of the woman. It is then ready to receive life. Disturbing it is a crime. When it develops further and becomes a lump, aborting it is a greater crime. When it acquires a soul and its creation is completed, the crime becomes more grievous. The crime reaches a maximum seriousness when it is committed after it (the foetus) is separated (from the mother) alive. (Al-Qaradawi Y, 1985: 202)

However, according to Islam, when the pregnancy threatens the life of the mother, the foetus may be aborted on the grounds of choosing a lesser evil. Economic reasons, however, do not justify abortion. To abort for economic reasons is lack of trust in God who is "the Provider of all means", and "The Best of Providers".

According to the Baha'i Faith, the soul of a person comes into being at conception. Consequently, the general principle is that abortion, merely for getting rid of an unwanted child, is absolutely wrong.

The Baha'i Faith, however, recognises that there are certain circumstances in which abortion may be justified. The matter is left on the consciences of those concerned who must, for example, weigh the medical advice on the case carefully (Hornby H, 1988: 344).

Abortion is an extremely sensitive moral issue which involves the destruction of innocent human life of the foetus. It is also likely to have adverse physical, psychological and moral consequences for a woman who commits it. First of all, complications such as excessive bleeding, infection, perforation of the uterus or the tearing of the cervix could follow an abortion, with future undesirable consequences. Some women even die in the process of abortion and those who survive it, sometimes suffer from miscarriage, premature birth or giving birth to deformed children.

If abortion causes infection, this could in turn result in infertility. Abortion may also cause psychological disorders because a mother who has aborted her child may always haunted by the death of that unborn child. It means, therefore, that a decision to abort should not be taken easily because of its adverse consequences.

On the issue of humanisation for the foetus, it is known that there is a process of growth, development and change during the course of a human pregnancy in the nine month gestation period, after fertilisation. As the foetus develops, there is an increasing degree of certainty that it has become a human being. A foetus, at any stage, if not a human being, at least it has human life.

The decision by an expectant mother to induce the termination of a pregnancy is often done regretfully under physical, social or economic pressure and in the absence of adequate social, psychological and spiritual support which used to be provided by the extended family in the African traditional setting. Things have changed and it is increasingly difficult to adhere to traditional norms and because of that not only justice should be considered in judging a case of abortion, but compassion, love, sympathy and understanding should be extended to a mother who desperately has taken a step she may live to regret.

Currently, Africa is experiencing radical changes in different spheres of life, including morality. There have been dramatic economic and social changes associated with urbanisation and industrialisation which militate against big families or even having one child. Another noteworthy development has been a fall in infant and general mortality rate without a corresponding fall in the birth rate. All these factors call for a change of attitude toward abortion. It is important that the consequences of not committing abortion, too, should be considered in evolving a relevant ethic of abortion.

Society should consider, for example, the problems associated with single parenthood, the social stigma and inconveniences in life which result from pre-marital pregnancy, the effects of a child which is a result of rape, the financial situation of a couple or of the expectant mother, the health and well-being of the existing children in the family and the expectant mother's professional considerations. The welfare and stability of the family are also important considerations in thinking about abortion. Each case of abortion, therefore, should be judged in its own circumstances. There is a need for readjustment and revaluation in moral thinking about abortion, keeping in mind the African respect for human life from conception.

Euthanasia

Although euthanasia, popularly known as 'mercy killing', is not as common in Africa as suicide or abortion, it is gaining acceptance. Euthanasia refers to the practice of killing or letting a person die for the purpose of putting an end to extreme pain or indignity in situations of imminent death. The motive is to save a person who will inevitably die from the prolongation of a miserable life.

As is the case with suicide, there is a distinction between active euthanasia which involves administering a drug or doing something else which will hasten the death of the patient and passive euthanasia. Passive euthanasia means allowing the suffering person to die by withholding any treatment that is capable of keeping him or her alive. Sometimes these means to sustain life, such as a respirator, are extraordinary and withdrawing them is often called "pulling the plug".

The advocates of euthanasia argue that when a person has an incurable and painful disease or has lost the capacity for normal human satisfactions such as the cultivation of interpersonal relations, creative employment or intellectual pursuit, life for him or her is meaningless and it should be terminated by some painless method to end his or her suffering. Examples which are often cited are irreversible comma; when a person is only living vegetatively and an incurable and painful disease such as cancer. Some people would like to extend euthanasia to a completely deteriorated personality; as in extremely mad people, a severely defective new born such as one born with a partial or total absence of the brain or in cases of extreme senility.

The aim of euthanasia in each of the above cases is to give the patient gentle and easy death. The argument is that in such a situation, although biological life continues, a person is permanently incapable of functioning in any recognisably human fashion and is, therefore, better off dead than alive. Advocates of euthanasia contend that in such situations, mercy and love are on the side of death and such a person should be assisted to die quickly and painlessly.

There is a difference between voluntary and non-voluntary euthanasia. Voluntary euthanasia refers to the gentle termination of life for which a person of sound mind asks, in the event of his or her becoming a victim of grievous accident or ravaging disease. Advocates of euthanasia include in a person's rights, a right to choose a dignified death instead of a degrading and disgusting end. They argue that death which is preceded or accompanied by severe and prolonged suffering causes anguish and affects the human psychological make-up and creates a bad end.

Some people do not accept this type of reasoning. They argue that certain actions are good or evil, irrespective of the motive or intention for which they are done, even apart from their consequences. To deliberately take a person's life is one such act and is regarded as homicide and wrong and so is asking for it.

There are even people who are of the view that it is morally acceptable, for the sake of the victim, to put to death a sick person without his or her consent by someone acting in private or public capacity, if the sick person is not in position to give that consent, but it is believed that he or she would have given it. This applies, among many cases, to grossly deformed or mentally defective babies. It would also apply to adults, especially those with terminal, painful or humiliating illness. In both cases a person is incapable of making a decision and she or he cannot, therefore, be consulted. This is what is known as non-voluntary euthanasia. The argument for this position is that death in such cases is in the sufferer's best interest and to give them a speedy and gentle release would be an act of merciful kindness to them.

Obviously those who object to voluntary euthanasia are even more so opposed to non-voluntary euthanasia. They argue that the natural inclination for everyone is to save life, not to end it and that euthanasia is unnatural because the will to live which is natural should be promoted, not weakened. Opponents of euthanasia in addition argue that doctors are not always right in their diagnosis and that in fact they are often wrong. For that reason people cannot always depend on the verdict of incurability by the doctor. The argument is that death being final, the error of euthanasia is too great to be risked. They also argue that diseases which were considered incurable at one time are now curable. According to them, new experiments and discoveries may in future treat what is regarded as incurable now and the benefit of the possibility should be on the side of life, not of death. They want to leave the options open. In any case, they argue, spontaneous remission sometimes occurs and many cases which were diagnosed as incurable with imminent death are known to have lived for a long time. They object to euthanasia because it leaves no room for such 'miraculous' recoveries.

Some people are so severely disabled either as a result of a congenital handicap, chronic illness, accident or from mental or physical deficiency that they do not have the capacity for normal human satisfactions. Worse still, they may be exposed to indignity. Many advocates of euthanasia argue that such people should be helped to "rest" from the misery of living.

Opponents of euthanasia argue that however seriously a person is deformed, she or he is still a human being with the corresponding innate, and inviolable right to life. There is also the question of determining the degree of deformity that one may call hopeless deserving euthanasia. The argument is that what one person may condemn as a hopeless deformity may be tolerated by another.

Already mentioned in African societies, life is so valued that killing a person is not allowed unless someone has been condemned or during the war. However, mercy killing is sometimes practised. If a person is fatally wounded during the war or when hunting, for example, it is morally acceptable for his colleague to kill him or her in order to save him from prolonged pain. In the past, wounded warriors who could not run from capture were killed or helped by their colleagues to die in order to save them from capture and torture.

The general Christian position is against all forms of euthanasia on the grounds that people were created by God and belong to him, therefore, they have no right to dispose of themselves. Christianity also teaches that the right to life is God given, and it is not in anyone's moral competence deliberately and directly to take the life of any innocent human being even with his or her consent. To do it, is regarded as an act of injustice to the person and an act of impiety toward God who gave the person life. For Christians, a person's death is the death willed for him or her by God, at the time God wills and in the manner He wills. Only God can say when one's years are completed and one's course towards Him is run (Daughters of St. Paul, 1984: 64).

It is also argued that it is everyone's duty to take care of God's property entrusted to his or her charge including souls and bodies. A person also has a duty to his or her neighbour and it is a duty to help and not to hinder him or her from attaining the end destined for him or her by God. On the point of compassion for those in severe pain, it is argued that true compassion is incompatible with injustice or impiety of euthanasia and suffering cannot be relieved at any cost.

The Christian position is that it is a denial of God's loving providence to assert, at any given time, that one's life can no longer serve any good purpose and that to take with deliberate intent the life of any innocent person, whether incurably sick or in good health, is to commit a grave sin of murder (Childress J, 1986: 211).

Islam does not accept euthanasia, either. According to Islam, no one may end life on his or her own whim and fancy. Islam teaches that to give and take life is the prerogative of Allah alone. All forms of euthanasia, including voluntary euthanasia, are forbidden.

The Baha'i Faith, too, does not permit any form of taking away of human life, including euthanasia. The Baha'i teaching is that God created human beings and it is up to him to take them at the time he, alone, chooses. Even voluntary euthanasia is prohibited in the Baha'i Faith.

Euthanasia is condemned by some people and supported by others. However, it is reasonable to say that withholding or withdrawing *extraordinary* means of life support such as a respirator, under specific conditions, especially with the consent of the patient, is morally acceptable.

Those caring for a sick person are expected to study the type of treatment to be used, its degree of complexity or risk, its cost and the possibilities of using it, and comparing these elements with the result that can be expected, taking into account the state of the sick person and his or her physical and moral resources. If keeping the person alive requires extraordinary means, if need be, these means may be withdrawn and a person allowed to die. This is more so when the means are too expensive or when they will not help the patient to improve, but they are just to stop him from dying.

It should be noted, however, that even when a person asks to be killed, this should not always be regarded as a genuine request to take seriously. This is because the pleas of a gravely ill person who may ask for death may not be a true desire for euthanasia. His or her request may be a case of an anguished plea for help and love (Daughters of St. Paul, 1984: 59). Since there are often genuine cases deserving help, such as a person who is trapped in a burning car, euthanasia should not be completely ruled out.

Domestic Violence
Violence at home takes different forms especially the violence by parents to children and between husband and wife. The most common, however, is the violence by men towards their wives, especially wife-beating. It is that form of violence that this section focusses on.

Traditionally in Africa beating one's wife was accepted as normal. In fact, it was regarded as abnormal, if provoked by his wife, a man did not beat her. Wife-beating is still common in many African countries, especially in southern Africa.

In most African societies, a wife was regarded as a junior partner and was disciplined by her husband when he believed that she was in the wrong. Nevertheless, this did not mean that a man could beat his wife without 'good reasons' or in a way he chose. There were certain faults which deserved discipline from a man, even a beating for that matter. These were many including not caring for children, failure to prepare food for the family or for the husband on time, showing disrespect to the husband or to the in-laws, violating taboos, and unfaithfulness.

When there was good reason to do so, a man beat his wife, but not severely to cause permanent bodily harm. Besides, a man was not supposed to hit his wife on certain parts of the body such as the head or breasts. He had to be selective when hitting her. A man who beat his wife very severely or on wrong parts was fined by his own family and, if the wife returned to her own people, the husband was warned and fined. He could even be beaten up by his brothers in-law.

On the grounds of the sacredness of life, it is wrong in Christian thinking for a man to beat his wife. "Thou shalt not kill" extends to any act which threatens life or the health of another person. Inflicting pain on another person violates God's commandment. It is also a violation of a greater commandment to love.

Beating one's wife also suggests disrespect for human dignity which is an inherent value of a person from which no one may deprive him or her. The church teaches that human beings are to be considered as entities in relation to God. Consequently, every human being, regardless of gender, is an object of reverence for other people.

According to Islam a woman must obey her husband. As the head of the family, a man has a right to correct his wife, when she misbehaves. He may even beat her, although he should do so with consideration. The Quran says:

> As to those women
> On whose part you fear
> Disloyalty and ill conduct
> Admonish them (first)
> (Next) Refuse to share their beds
> And last) beat them (lightly)
> (4:34)

Although it is permitted in Islam, wife beating, is not advisable because cruelty is condemned.

The Baha'is believe that men beat their wives because they regard them as inferior and subordinates, not as equals. The Baha'i Faith teaches the equality of men and women, with equal rights, privileges, and responsibilities. It follows, therefore, that neither sex should oppress, exploit or mistreat the other. In family relations the Faith emphasises concord, mutual understanding and unity and advocates that each member should uphold the rights of the other members. Abdul Baha stressed harmony in the family and succinctly condemned wife-beating in the following words:

If the broad structure of society is to remain intact, resolute efforts, including medical ones, as necessary, should be made to curb acts of aggression within families, particularly their extreme forms of wife beating and child abuse by parents.
(Hornby H, 1988: 221-222)

Wife-beating is a multi-dimensional moral problem. It involves violence against a person, oppression of women, and unfairness. Men and women are created equal and there should not be a situation of one partner disciplining another. For a man to claim a right to discipline a wife is to treat her as an inferior person. Beating her is doubly bad because it is to use violence against her. Wife beating is cruel, dehumanising, and a violation of a wife's dignity and rights.

Chapter Six

SEX OUTSIDE MARRIAGE

Sexual ethics refers to moral rules and principles pertaining to relations between sexes, especially with reference to mutual attraction and to the satisfaction of the desires resulting from it.

Norms on sex
Different societies, groups, and religions have norms which they apply in judging what is appropriate or inappropriate sexual behaviour and these vary considerably. These norms may broadly be grouped into two camps namely conventional and liberal positions.

According to conventionalists sexual activity is only morally appropriate within the bounds of marriage. Both pre and extra marital sexual activity are regarded as immoral.

Conventionalists base their position on the 'social utility theory' and the 'natural law theory'. According to the social utility theory, a stable family is absolutely necessary for the proper raising of children and the consequent welfare of society. The argument is that limiting sex to marriage is a necessary condition for forming and maintaining stable family units on the grounds that availability of sex within marriage reinforces the loving relationship between husband and wife, the exclusive availability of it in marriage leads most people to get married and to stay married, and the unavailability of extra marital sex keeps marriage strong (Mappes T, 1982:199).

With regard to the natural law theory, actions are morally appropriate in so far as they accord with the essence of human nature. On those grounds, it is argued that the emission of semen ought to be ordered in such a way that it will result in the production and proper upbringing of offsprings. Conventionalists argue that every emission of semen in such a way that the generation of offspring cannot follow is contrary to human nature and if it is done deliberately, even within marriage, it is wrong. On those grounds, oral and anal intercourse, masturbation, artificial birth control and homosexuality or lesbianism are condemned. It is also regarded as contrary to the good of man if semen is emitted under conditions that generation could result but the proper upbringing of the offspring would be prevented. Thus, sex outside marriage is regarded as immoral.

On the other hand, liberals reject the view that non-marital sex is *per se* immoral. They argue that sexual activity is just one type of human activity and should be judged in the same way that any other human activity is subject to moral appraisal. This, they contend, should be with reference to relevant, universally agreed, general moral rules and principles. According to them, if a sexual activity violates one of those rules then it is immoral but if it does not, there is nothing wrong with it (Mappes T, 1982:201)

It is a moral rule, for example, not to inflict harm on another innocent person. A sexual activity which does this is regarded as immoral. On these grounds seduction of a minor would be condemned because it harms her psychologically. Rape, too, would be condemned because it inflicts both physical and psychological pain on the victim.

Another example is the rule that one should not use another person for his or her own ends. On these grounds, sexual activity without voluntary informed consent would be condemned as wrong. An example of this is deception, when, for example, a man deceives a girl that he intends to marry her when he does not, and on those grounds the girl consents to having a sexual affair with him. Sex by coercion is also regarded as immoral. Although in such a situation there is consent, and the person is informed, he or she does it out of fear.

Provided the above rules and other general moral principles are not violated, the liberals believe that non-marital sex is morally acceptable. Sexual intercourse may be a result of mutual love or affection between two adults or merely a mutual desire for sexual satisfaction. It may be hetero or homo or it may even be mutual masturbation. All these forms of sexual activity are acceptable as long as they do not violate any general moral principle.

Liberals would condemn adultery only on the grounds that it is breach of the promise to be faithful to one another. If marriage did not include a pledge of sexual exclusivity, as it is not in traditional African marriages, then, according to liberals, there is nothing wrong with extra-marital sexual relationships.

In African religions, sex occupies an important place in social and religious lives of the people and it is associated with many beliefs, practices and taboos. Sex is respected as a channel for procreation, a means to regain the immortality which was lost in the remote past. So sex is of tremendous religious significance with taboos attached to it. It is believed among the Nyakyusa of Tanzania, for example, that sexual fluid is so sacred that it is harmful to babies and a woman keeps away from her husband during the nursing period and when she gets involved in a sexual act, she must wash herself thoroughly before getting in touch with her baby. Among the Banyankore, it is believed that adultery committed when a person is in the process of building a house causes death for the partner when they enter the new house. A cleansing ritual is necessary before they occupy the house to avert the danger. Among the Bakiga of Uganda, a parent to intentionally show his or her genital organ to the child with the intention of cursing him or her is the most efficacious method. Sex has both biological and social functions. It may even be indulged in for pleasure or even as an expression of hospitality. Whatever uses it is put to, sex in African societies has functions which are held sacred and must be indulged in according to what is regarded as a proper way. There are many sexual offences such as fornication, adultery, rape, homosexuality or incest which are punishable by the society and the ancestors.

Christianity postulates that sexuality and sexual differences are God's creation and they are, therefore, good and sacred (Gen. 1:27). Sex is, therefore, to be used properly and responsibly. A general Christian principle is that sex should take place only within the framework of marriage. Sexual intercourse is for procreation purposes and protection against sin. Sex, procreation and marriage are understood in terms of the welfare of the community rather than the individual's desires or satisfaction. In conventional Christian ethics, the ideal sexual act is hetero-sexual, potentially procreative, expressive of the permanent and monogamous relationship, facilitating the nurture of Children and creating domestic and social stability (Childress J, 1986: 579). Recently, however, there has been a change of attitude and the value and subjective experience of the individual is stressed over and above the procreative purpose of sex. Satisfaction of sexual desire or drive and the expression of a positive relation between partners are recognised as positive functions of sex.

The Bible confirms this view. In the bible sex is not seen only in terms of reproduction but is ordained also for personal and social partnership (Gen. 2:18-25). There is emphasis on both love and procreation in sexual activity. Sex is a gift from God to be used for pleasure and joy (Songs 6:10-16, 7ff, 8ff).

The emphasis on the affective and enjoyable aspects of sex has led some Christians to justify pre or extra marital sex that express love (Childress J, 1986:583). In addition, homosexuality is coming into debate in proportion to the declining emphasis on procreation and the rise in emphasis on interpersonal sexual communion and pleasure as the functions of sex (Childress J, 1986 :580). Some Christian groups, however, still regard sex for self-satisfaction as a deviation from its intended purpose.

Islam teaches that Allah created people to be his representatives on earth in order that they may populate and rule it. So the human race has an obligation to perpetuate itself. Allah placed certain appetites and impulses in people so that they may be impelled toward the various activities which guarantee their survival. One of them is the sexual drive. The sexual appetite, which is for the purpose of the survival of humanity, is a strong driving force in a human being which demands satisfaction and fulfilment.

Islam, however, does not accept the satisfaction of one's sexual needs freely with whomever is available and whenever one pleases. Nor does it allow

Muslims to suppress and try to annihilate the sexual drive. Both approaches, according to Islam, are contrary to Allah's plan and purpose. Islam, therefore, advocates regulation of the satisfaction of the sexual urge, allowing it to operate within certain limits, and only through lawful marriage (Al-Qaradawi Y, 1985 :149).

The Baha'i Faith recognises the value of the sexual impulse, but condemns what it regards as its illegitimate and improper expression such as free love, companionate marriage and similar other non-marital sexual relations. The only legitimate place of sexual activity is within marriage.

The sexual urge is one of the most powerful human inclinations and its fulfilment is perhaps the most enjoyable and absorbing of human experiences. It means, therefore, that sex is both a sensitive and important subject in the lives of people and to enjoy it, or not to do so, deserves serious consideration. Sexual emotions, like other emotions such as jealousy, anger and hatred can lead a person into danger if they are not put to proper use. People have to make an effort to learn to cope with sexual emotions and feelings in order to keep them under control both within and outside marriage. It is important to express sexual feelings but this should be consistent with African traditions; at the right time and place and with the right person.

Since sexual activity involves a second party, it should not be regarded as a mere act of pleasure or a mechanical activity which tends to dehumanise those involved in it, by treating the other person as a sex object. Sex should also be indulged in with seriousness, knowing and prepared for the consequences from it, since irresponsible sex could result in unwanted pregnancies, unplanned children, abortion and sexually transmitted diseases including AIDS. These are moral problems which cause misery and suffering.

Fornication
Fornication is the voluntary sexual intercourse between unmarried persons. Whereas liberals regard all sex with free informed consent of adults as permissible, some groups and religions condemn fornication as immoral.

As a general principle, in African religions, sex before marriage is discouraged and severely punished. A girl, for example, is expected to be chaste until marriage. For that reason, virginity is highly valued and rewarded. In most African societies, girls are taught to protect their virginity until marriage and never to allow a man to violate it.

Among the Swazi, for example, a girl who is engaged for marriage is allowed to visit her fiance for a number of days *(kujuma)* and the two stay in the boy's house *(lilawu)* and may even share a bed. However, no sexual intercourse between them is allowed. The two may kiss and fondle but under no excuse are they supposed to have sexual intercourse. If the boy is strongly overcome by sexual urge, he makes love to his fiance between her thighs, a form of masturbation. A girl who accepts her boy friend to make love to her and loses her virginity loses her respect and is a source of embarrassment to her parents and age mates. Similar views about premarital sex exist among many other African societies.

Christian sexual ethics focusses on adultery and there is little said about fornication in the Scriptures. However, the general position is that fornication is morally wrong because it is a misuse of one's body which is the temple of God, violates the virtue of purity (1 Cor. 6:12-20), and is forbidden by God (ex. 22:16; Mt. 15:19). Sexual intercourse for fun or pleasure falls short of the Christian ideal that sexual intercourse is best expressed in the union of marriage. Sexual urge is regarded as lawful if it is directed to complete and permanent commitment to each other (1 Cor. 6:6-12) and such commitment, according to Christianity, only exists in marriage.

In Islam, sex outside marriage is prohibited. In addition, the Islamic principle is that if something is prohibited, anything which leads to it is prohibited as well. In this regard, anything leading to fornication or making it attractive such as seductive clothing, private meetings of a man and a woman or casual meetings between them, the depiction of nudity, pornographic literature, obscene songs, and other things which are conducive to fornication are all prohibited (Al-Qaradawi Y, 1985:28). There is no justification for pre-marital sex in Islam.

Fornication is also forbidden in the Baha'i Faith. The Faith teaches that chastity should be practised by both sexes because it is highly commendable morally and because it is the only way to a happy and successful marital life. The other reason why fornication is forbidden is that it sometimes leads to the birth of illegitimate children, single-parent homes, child-raising by grandparents, emotional insecurity, and the spread of venereal diseases (Lowell J, 1987:76). Thus sexual relationships of any form, outside lawful marriage are not allowed.

Before marriage, Baha'is are required to be absolutely chaste. Young men and women should only establish bonds of comradeship and love which are founded on spiritual values and not on the physical side of mating. The Baha'i Faith teaches that the Baha'i youths should be taught self-control which, when exercised, has a salutary effect on the development of character and personality in general and that they should be advised or even encouraged to get married when still young, when they are still in possession of their physical vigour. This will help them against the temptation of sexual immorality.

There are many reasons why people get involved in pre-marital sexual intercourse which have a bearing on the morality of it. These include the mere desire to have fun, "trial sex" to get to know each other with some view to possible marriage, to confirm the fertility of the couples before marriage, or to grow into intimacy with a view to a satisfactory marriage. There are also cases where marital commitment is almost complete on both sides, but the marriage ceremony is prevented by causes outside the couple's control such as church laws or payment of bride-gifts. This shows that the different forms of pre-marital sex cannot be simply judged as equally wrong, but a variable morality has to be applied.

It is difficult, for example, to agree with the libertines, who claim that sex is, like food, a natural necessity and, therefore, may be indulged in as one wishes. Sex, unlike food or drink, affects another person and sometimes families. It is also difficult to agree that sex by a couple who are deeply and personally committed to each other is equally morally wrong. One believes that the sexual intercourse of a man and a woman who are totally committed to one another, and only circumstances are delaying their public proclamation of that commitment to each other, has a similar character of sexual intercourse within marriage. Whereas marital intention, affection and commitment which are not yet contracted can be easily revoked, seriousness and personal commitment to one another are important considerations in assessing the morality of a particular sexual act because of the possible outcome of it.

The view that sex outside marriage is wrong because it could lead to the procreation of a child and that to procreate a child outside marriage is an injustice to it and to society seems to be a weak argument since with the availability of contraceptives, there is the possibility of near certainty that no child will be conceived. The morality of the use of contraceptives will be discussed in the next chapter. A very serious consideration is that self-control in sexual matters before marriage is a good training for the self-control that is required in marriage, for example when the partner is sick or away from home. Self-control in sexual matters is also important in order to avoid undesirable consequences.

Adultery
Adultery refers to sexual intercourse between a married person and someone else, other than the spouse. As we shall see below, in most African societies where a man is free to take a second wife or sleep with his unmarried sisters in-law, adultery as a moral issue is understood differently. In African religions, sexual intercourse is governed by regulations and taboos which should not be violated. One of the violations of sexual regulations is adultery.

However, in African religious understanding adultery refers to sexual intercourse between a married woman or man with another partner, other than the spouse, who custom does not permit her or him to have sexual intercourse with. Some forms of extra-marital sex are acceptable in African societies.

There are societies, for example, where sex is used as an expression of hospitality. Among Abahima of Uganda, when a man visits a very close friend or brother, the host may give his wife to his guest and the two sleep together. Sexual intercourse between them is not regarded as immoral. It is tolerable for a man to indulge in sexual intercourse with the wife or wives of his brother. If a man finds his brother in bed with his wife and complains or fights him, the elders will blame or punish the husband, not the 'intruding' brother. Mbiti also reports that where the age group system is very strong, among the Masai for example, members of the same group who were initiated together are entitled to have sexual relations with the wives of fellow members (Mbiti, 1969:147).

None of these forms of extra-marital sex is regarded as immoral. There are other acceptable extra marital forms of sex which are regarded as normal and proper. However, extra-marital sexual intercourse outside the acceptable forms is prohibited. When committed by the wife, it may lead to divorce.

In Christianity, adultery is a violation of the sixth commandment, "You shall not commit adultery" (Ex. 20:14) together with the tenth commandment, "You shall not covet your neighbour's wife" (Ex. 20:17). In the Old Testament, the penalty for adultery was death for both partners (Lev. 20:10; Deut. 22:22; Ex. 20:14; Lev. 18:20; Deut. 5:18). The severity of the punishment suggests that adultery was viewed not just as a private violation of the spouse's right to exclusive sexual enjoyment of the partner, but also as a serious social threat to the fabric of society.

Adultery is also condemned in the New Testament (Mt. 5:27-28; Jn. 8:3-11) and Jesus extends it to the inner thoughts and desires where moral offence has its origins. Jesus emphasises the spirit of adultery "You have heard that it is said, 'You shall not commit adultery'. But I say to you that everyone who looks at a woman lustfully has already committed adultery with her in his heart" (Mt. 5:27-28; Jn. 8:3-11). It is reasonable to suppose that this also applies to a woman who looks at a man lustfully. All thinking, speaking, and conduct, which are inconsistent with, and lead to a destruction of, marriage are regarded as adultery.

Divorcing and marrying another wife or husband is also regarded as adultery against the first partner (Mk. 4:20). It is believed that, by equating divorce with adultery, Jesus exemplifies God's original order in creation (Mt. 19:4ff; Gen 1:27, 2:24), an order that is destined to be restored (Mt. 19:28).

Islam regards adultery as a shameful deed and an evil, opening the way to other evils such as confusion of lineage, child abuse, the breaking-up of families, bitterness in relationships, the spread of venereal diseases, and general laxity in morals. It strongly condemns adultery and an adulterous man or woman is to be severely punished. According to the Quran:

> The woman and the man
> Guilty of adultery or fornication
> Flog each of them
> With a hundred stripes (24:2)

The Quran commands sexual purity for men and women at all times before, during and after the dissolution of marriage. A Muslim who has been found guilty of adultery is not allowed to marry a chaste muslim woman or man (24:3).

A man or woman must take precaution to avoid all things which might lead him or her to adultery or wrong thoughts and sexual feelings. Islam, for example, prohibits looking at a member of the opposite sex with desire, "for the eye is the key to the feelings, and the look is a messenger of desire, carrying the message of fornication or adultery" (Al-Qaradawi Y, 1985:151). All forms of dress, movements, speech or conduct which may arouse sexual feelings are regarded as adulterous and, therefore, prohibited.

Adultery is uncompromisingly forbidden in the Baha'i Faith. For the Faith, the proper use of sex instinct is the natural right of every individual and it is for this reason and purpose that the institution of marriage has been established. Outside marital life there can be no acceptable or healthy use of the sex impulse. Adultery, according to the Baha'i Faith is harmful to the individuals involved in it and to the society in which they live. After marriage, a Baha'i is required to be absolutely faithful to one's partner, and this means being faithful in all sexual acts.

The major issues associated with adultery are injustice and breach of promise. It, therefore, becomes controversial whether adultery remains immoral when the person has the consent of the spouse or when it is initiated by him or her as is the case when it is done for hospitality. There are also cases, as in traditional Swazi marriages, when there is no promise by the husband to his wife of exclusive sexual intercourse. Right from the beginning of marriage the wife knows that the husband may have sexual intercourse with her younger unmarried sisters or may marry a second wife. In this case, there is no breach of promise which is associated with adultery.

Modern technology has introduced other questions such as the morality of a man donating semen to a woman other than his wife. All these are issues which deserve serious consideration. In all matters, discipline, self-control, fairness and prudence are called into question. So is respect for the feelings of one's partner.

Prostitution

Prostitution is the practice of engaging in sexual activity for immediate compensation in favours, money or other valuables, in which affection and emotional attachment are minimal or completely absent, and in which the selection of sexual partners is relatively indiscriminate (Childress, 1986 :512). The most common form of prostitution is of women serving male customers although one also comes across men selling to women (Gigolos), men selling to fellow men (hustlers) and occasionally women selling to fellow women. Hetero-sexual male prostitution is less common and indirect, taking the form of 'sugar mummy' syndrome in older women, especially tourists, the services of the young men. Homosexual prostitution is still rare in Africa.

Whereas prostitution may take place in a brothel, an establishment where prostitutes reside, usually supervised by an older female there are other methods of prostitution such as call-girl or independent prostitution.

African religions are silent about prostitution because it is a new phenomenon in Africa, resulting from foreign influences associated with Western materialism, urbanisation and commercialism. However, from the general position of African religions which regards sex as sacred, to be used primarily for procreation and upbringing of children or for cementing community ties, prostitution which falls out of those two functions, would be regarded as improper to say the least.

In principle, Christianity regards prostitution as wrong and immoral. In the Old Testament, prostitution is generally condemned (Lev. 19:29) but there is some degree of tolerance of female prostitution. The New Testament, too, condemns it (1 Cor. 6:15-17). As a result, the church from its beginnings has condemned all forms of prostitution but tolerated it at times as "the lesser evil" of other evils such as rampant lust, rape, adultery and homosexual practices which would result if prostitution were abolished. Nevertheless, the church has continued to condemn prostitution on the ground that "an appropriate understanding of sexuality calls for the investment of the total person in the act of sexual intimacy in relationships marked by fidelity and commitment to the wholeness of the partner-qualities that are absent in the typical prostitute-client activity" (Childress J, 1986: 513).

Islam condemns prostitution and forbids any Muslim, male or female, to earn money by it. According to Islam, there is no sound reason, not even need or distress, which can justify prostitution. Islam also prohibits earning money by sexually exciting dancing or any other erotic activity such as suggestive or obscene songs, provocative dramas and any other activity which tempts, excites and leads towards unlawful sex.

In the Baha'i Faith sexual relationships, of any form, outside marriage are not permitted. Since prostitution involves sex outside marriage it is consequently prohibited. So are all manners of promiscuity.

After considering the advantages and disadvantages of prostitution, a key question which is usually asked is whether prostitution should be tolerated or suppressed by the law. Although this is not a moral question, it has moral implications. In some societies, prostitution has been tolerated and it is an accepted social phenomenon. The argument for toleration is that governments should respect people's autonomy and not impose penalties on private, consensual sexual behaviour by adults. They also argue that anti-prostitution laws are ineffective, selectively applied and difficult and expensive to enforce (Childress J, 1986 :513). In other countries, prostitution is tolerated, but controlled for example, by licensing brothels which can be supervised from a health point of view. In yet others, prostitution is illegal and criminal. Individual soliciting is also a crime.

Whereas anti prostitution laws are often seen as an effort to prevent or reduce exploitation of women, it seems that legalising it decreases the exploitation of prostitutes and reduces crime associated with it.

There are many people who argue that prostitution should be tolerated as a lesser evil without which adultery, rape and other evils would increase. This, however, should not include childhood prostitution especially of teenager runaways from disintegrating families and school children who are too young to make independent decisions.

The use of paid sexual surrogates for therapeutic reasons is another difficult issue which is not discussed here because it is rare in the African context. However, it should be noted that in moral decision making or judgement, the motives, intentions and consequences involved in the act are important considerations.

Homosexuality
Homosexuality refers to a predominant and persistent sexual attraction toward members of the same sex (Childress J, 1986: 271). There is a distinction between homosexual orientation and homosexual activity. Homosexual activities may be engaged in for money by people who are predominantly heterosexual. On

the other hand, a person with homosexual orientation may refrain from homosexual activity or may remain celibate. As a moral problem, homosexuality usually refers to sexual relations with a member of the same sex.

Men homosexuals are popularly known as gay men and female homosexuals as lesbians. In both cases, homosexuality is generally, up to now, regarded as a divergence from normal sexual development or orientation. However, current knowledge of homosexuality seems to reveal that the predominant homosexual orientation does not carry with it any clinical pathology except psychological and behavioral problems stemming from social oppression, problems that are similar to those found in other socially oppressed groups (Childress J, 1986 :272).

Homosexuality, in a typical African traditional setting, was extremely rare. Only few members of the affluent and royal families occasionally practised it. Consequently, African religions do not say much about it. All one can say is that homosexuality does not fulfil the traditional functions of sex as perceived by African religions. External influences, however, have popularised homosexuality among ordinary people and more and more young men and women are getting drawn to it. This may be an indication that, even before foreign influence, the orientation to homosexuality was existing but suppressed.

Homosexual acts are forbidden in the Old Testament (Lev. 18:22). The destruction of Sodom and Gommorah (Gen. 19) often is attributed to homosexual acts. According to the Old Testament male homosexuality is punishable by death (Lev. 20:13). The New Testament, too, condemns homosexuality as unnatural (Rom. 1:26-27). According to the Bible, homosexuality, like greed or adultery, precludes inheritance of the kingdom of God (1 Cor. 6:9-10; 1 Tim. 1:9-10). These passages, however, raise hermeneutical questions beyond us to debate here.

Islam regulates sexual drive and prohibits what it regards as illicit sexual relations and all ways which lead to them. It also prohibits all that it regards as sexual deviation, including homosexuality. Islam regards homosexuality as a perverted act which is a reversal of the natural order, a corruption of human sexuality and a crime against the rights of members of the opposite sex.

According to Islam, the spread of homosexuality in society disrupts its natural life pattern and makes those who practise it slaves to their lusts, depriving them of decent taste, decent morals, and a decent manner of living (Al-Qaradawi Y, 1985: 169). Homosexuality is also condemned in the Quran (26: 165-166).

In the writings of the Baha'i Faith, homosexuality is condemned. Homosexual relations of any kind are not permissible. The Baha'i Faith teaches that homosexuality is a distortion of human nature which should be controlled and overcome, but not reconciled to the Baha'i way of life. However, according to the Baha'i Faith homosexuality can have medical aspects, and in such cases recourse should be medical assistance. The Faith recognises that it may be a hard struggle for a homosexual to control his or her desires, but so also can be the struggle of a heterosexual person to control his or her sexual desires. Self-control is, therefore, strongly recommended.

Ethical reflections on homosexuality should take into account certain considerations. There is a general agreement, for example, that basic sexual orientation becomes relatively fixed in early childhood, usually by the ages of five to seven, quite apart from the individual's choice. This indicates that a person is not morally responsible for his or her sexual orientation since he or she does not choose it. Efforts to reorient adult sexual preference may change certain sexual social behaviour, but do not usually have significant or lasting effect upon the feelings, desires, and sexual fantasies of a person (Childress J, 1986: 271-2). If this is the case, a person cannot be blamed for his or her homosexual orientation or for not changing it. Apparently, most people are neither exclusively heterosexual nor exclusively homosexual. What most people have is a predominant tendency toward one of those two orientations. All these factors need to be taken into consideration when judging homosexual acts. The African values of community and toleration should be practised even in the case of homosexuals.

Masturbation
Masturbation is the obtaining of sexual pleasure by self-stimulation. It may or may not result in ejaculation. It seems to be a common practice, especially among unmarried men, for a man to relieve himself of sexual tension by self-masturbation. Women, too, masturbate and mutual masturbation is practised by married people, as a form of fore play or for sexual satisfaction.

It is said that masturbatory activities may begin as early in life as the second year, when a child discovers pleasurable sensations on touching relevant parts of his or her body. This may continue into adulthood. Masturbation also occurs in some adults, both male and female, who have no other sexual outlet.

Medical research, so far, does not consider masturbation physically or emotionally harmful nor is it considered a symptom of an illness, unless it becomes a compulsion beyond wilful control.

Immorality in African ethical thought refers to a disruption of fellowship. Masturbation being an individual and personal act does not bother people in African societies. However, sexual fluids make a person impure and call for cleansing. A person who masturbates, when discovered is cleansed and warned not to do it again. This seems to be more of religious rather than ethical concern because emphasis is put on defilement and impurity, rather than the effects of the act on society.

Christianity teaches that sexual pleasure is designed to occur within the context of marriage only. Any sexual activity which has no potential for procreation or which is outside the framework of marriage is not acceptable. However, there has not been any outright condemnation of masturbation in the Bible or by the church. The silence could be interpreted to mean toleration.

As a general principle, and under normal circumstances, masturbation is not allowed by Islam. The Quran prohibits any sexual craving outside marriage (23:5-7). Masturbation, according to Islam, is such a craving. Masturbation, however, may be permitted if it is done in order to avoid committing fornication or adultery, which are regarded as greater evils in Islam. However, Muslims who masturbate to avoid the evils of fornication and adultery, are cautioned not to do it excessively or to make it a habit. Muslims are also advised to use more noble and spiritual means to cultivate self-control such as fasting or prayer which nurture will power. The solution to the problem of masturbation, according to Islam, is to marry or get married.

The Baha'i Faith teaches that masturbation is not a proper use of the sexual instinct and it is prohibited. No sexual act can be considered lawful unless performed between lawfully married persons. The Baha'i youth and those with a tendency for masturbation are to be taught the lesson of self-control.

It should be noted that morality presupposes action which is harmful to a person or to others. Only acts which are harmful to an individual or which affect others, for good or ill are of moral significance and since masturbation is not such an act, it is debatable whether it is a moral issue in cases of single people. It is up to an individual to decide whether to do it or not. For married people, masturbation is a moral concern because it affects the sexual life of the couple.

Sexism

Sexism is the assumption of the inherent superiority of one sex over the other. Some of the characteristics of sexism are treating or portraying the opposite sex in a demeaning fashion, regarding the opposite sex as subordinate, referring to persons of the opposite sex in stereo typed terms and exerting sexual power over a person of the opposite sex. Sexism is often magnified when it exists with other forms of discrimination and oppression such as racism, ageism, classism, heterosexism and tribalism. The main manifestations of sexism are sexual harassment, sexual assault and the worst form of it is rape. Either of these, however, may exist in a non-sexist situation or for non-sexist reasons.

Sexual harassment refers to unwanted and usually persistent sexual comments, looks, jokes, suggestions or physical contact which the person, who receives them, finds them objectionable, offensive and a cause of discomfort. Sexual harassment may take a form of assault.

Sexual assault is any unwanted act of a sexual nature imposed by one person upon an other which involves physical contact. The most common forms of sexual assault are touching and fondling and the worst form of it is, perhaps, rape.

Rape refers to sexual intercourse with a person without his or her consent. This could be done by force, fraudulent, or other means. In most cases women are the victims of rape. Though men too, may be raped by homosexuals and to a lesser extent by women rapists.

Sexual assault or rape are condemned by African religions. Rape, in particular, constitutes a very serious sexual offence. If a person is found guilty of rape, he is dealt with severely. He may be whipped, fined a number of cows or even stoned to death. Africans are sensitive to any departure from the accepted sexual norm. This is because as Mbiti notes, any sexual offence upsets the smooth relationships of the community, which includes those who have already departed (Mbiti, 1969:148).

The Christian commandment to love ones neighbour as oneself provides a Christian position on all forms of sexual harassment, assault or rape. They are all condemned as evil. Besides, since in most cases, this involves a person who is not a marriage partner, principles concerning fornication and adultery apply.

Sexual harassment, assault and rape are strictly prohibited in Islam. Any form of illicit sexual relations between a man and a woman or any step that leads to it is prohibited. As we noted earlier on, a Muslim may not even look at a member of the opposite sex with desire or touch her. It is reported that Prophet Muhammad said, "It is better for one of you to be pricked in the head with an iron than to touch a woman whom it is unlawful to touch" (Al-Qaradawi Y, 1985: 165).

Lechery and all forms of sexual vices are clearly forbidden in the Baha'i Faith. Kitab Aqdas condemns 'Zina" and one of the forms of zina is when the illicit sexual intercourse is performed through force or violence.

Whoever sexually harasses, assaults or rapes another remains morally responsible regardless of the environmental circumstances. It is never acceptable to use force in sexual relationships. No one has a right to pressure another for sex, not even to one's husband or wife. In some African societies there is a need to change men's attitudes toward sexuality especially the attitude of regarding women as sex objects. Changing sexist attitudes will go a long way to reducing sexual harassment, assault and even rape.

Rape is a particularly serious moral issue which violates the victim's body, dignity and right of self-determination. It may also have long-term negative effects on the victim affecting his or her self-confidence, sexuality and interpersonal relationships. In some cases, rape victims become pregnant leading to abortion or a life long rejection of the resultant child. The victim may also be infected with venereal diseases. So, whether accompanied by physical violence or not, rape is likely to cause stress to the victim.

The situation is worsened by the fact that very often victims of rape do not report it because of the social stigma attached to it in many societies and because often successful prosecution is difficult if the victim is not a virgin, if it is done when one is asleep or if there is no struggle because the victim was dosed first. The fear to reveal rape increases the victim's frustration and stress.

Even for married couples, a man has an obligation to respect the woman's sexuality. Sexual intercourse should take place when the man is sure that the response to his advances is definitely positive. In its absence, a man should not make the assumption that intercourse is acceptable.

It is wrong to believe that "when a woman says 'no' she means 'yes'". In those societies where a woman is brought up to say no even when she means yes, women should not give ambiguous responses to men in sexual matters. It is not proper, either, to make assumptions about a woman's behaviour or dress. Men often assume that women who drink a lot, dress in ways regarded as provocative automatically wants sex. Nor is it right to assume that because a woman has had sex with man before, she is willing to have it with him again. Also fondling or kissing do not automatically mean acceptance of sexual intercourse: a woman has a right to accept one and refuse the other.

Chapter Seven
MARRIAGE

Different societies and religious groups define marriage differently and these definitions determine their ethics of marriage. One definition of marriage, for example, is that it is a voluntary union for life of a man and a woman for purposes of founding a family. If this definition is accepted as a correct one, polygamy would be regarded as wrong. So would be the marriage of a minor, or arranged or forced marriage, homosexual marriage and trial marriage. Indeed, each of these forms of marriage creates moral problems for some people. Even whether to marry or not is a moral issue in some societies.

Celibacy
Celibacy refers to acceptance of an unmarried state by an adult who has resolved, or is bound by a vow, not to marry. The term, however, is commonly used to mean acceptance of a single state for religious reasons. In Africa, it is mainly Christian groups, and more particularly the Roman Catholic churches, which practise celibacy, but it is a practice which is found in many other religious traditions of the world, including Hinduism and Buddhism.

It is generally agreed that an individual, as an autonomous being has a right to choose the type of life he or she wants to live, as long as it does not deprive others of their rights or hurt them. On these grounds, it is argued that a person may choose not to marry. Another school of thought, however, rejects the view that a person is free to marry or not to marry. It is argued that a person has an obligation to marry in order to continue the chain of life. Not to marry is regarded as a failure to perform one's duties to society.

In African religions, one of the important duties of any member of the community is to marry in order to have children. Marriage is an important affair and the focus of existence; the point where the dead, the living and those yet to be born meet. It is thus a duty and a requirement. As Mbiti notes, "he who does not participate in it is a curse to the community, he is a rebel and a law breaker, he is not only abnormal but 'under-human'" (Mbiti, 1969:133). A normal person, and under normal circumstances, has a moral obligation to marry and not to do so wins a person social disapproval.

Different societies have different ways and customs of dealing with a person who does not get married. Among the Batoro, for example, if a person, of marrying age, dies without getting married, people beat up his or her body with a thorny bush to show that an unmarried person does not receive respect from the community. A similar practice among the Swazi is to push a maize comb in his or her anus before burial. There are many other practices which show that celibacy is totally discouraged and regarded as a failure to perform one's social, biological and religious duties.

In the early history of the church, celibacy was practised by monks who lived ascetic lives in caves and other isolated places. In the ordinary life of the church, only celibates were selected for high offices out of reverence for ascetism. Bishops were required to be celibate, and if already married, to separate from their wives. This tradition has continued in the Eastern churches. Some Western churches, too, demanded celibacy from their clerics, but the reformers rejected compulsory celibacy. After the Reformation, only the Roman Catholic church requires its priests and bishops to be celibate. In the Orthodox churches only bishops may not marry, but the priests may.

According to the Scriptures, service and devotion to God may be rendered better in an unmarried state. Jesus recommends celibacy for divine service and service to society, but leaves it optional (Mt. 19:12). Paul, too, preferred and recommended it (1 Cor. 7:27; 32-34). There are several other references in the Bible supporting celibacy (Mt. 10: 34-37; Mt. 12 : 46-50; Mt. 19: 12; Lk. 11:27ff; Lk. 18: 29ff). However, celibacy is recommended only when a person can exercise self-control. If he or she cannot, it is better for him or her to marry than "to be aflame with passion" (1 Cor. 7:8-9). Besides, marriage is regarded as a divine institution which is necessary for the perpetuation of the human race.

In Islam celibacy is not permitted. Islam teaches that the sexual instinct should not be suppressed and its functioning should not be annihilated. Islam regards an attempt to frustrate and annihilate the natural appetite for sex contrary to Allah's plan and purpose for humanity. It is also seen as being in conflict with the course of the natural order which requires the use of this appetite for the continuity of humanity.

According to Islam, if marriage is not undertaken, the sexual instinct does not play its role in the continuation of the human specie. Islam, therefore, prohibits celibacy and the shunning of women (Al-Qaradawi Y, 1985:149). Remaining celibate or renouncing worldly activity, even for the sake of devoting oneself to the worship and service of Allah, are prohibited. In addition, marriage is obligatory for everyone who can marry (5:90) in order to protect one's chastity and purity and not to fall into sin.

The Baha'i Faith teaches that the institution of marriage was established as the channel of rightful expression of the sexual impulse. To be married, therefore, is highly desirable and recommended. Nevertheless, marriage in the Baha'i Faith is not the central purpose in life. Therefore, if for some reason a person has to wait a long time before finding a spouse, or if ultimately he or she must remain single, it does not mean that he or she is unable to fulfil his or her life's purpose. So celibacy is discouraged, but not prohibited.

Marriage is so complex, important, and delicate that it should be undertaken freely and with great care. Yet some people marry by force because their parents want them to do so, because it is a tradition to marry at a certain age, or because they have become, or made someone, pregnant. Whereas such a marriage could succeed, chances are that it will not and this may result in misery not only for the couple, but also for the children resulting from that marriage and the families involved. It is better to remain single than to enter marriage without mutual love and commitment. Some people forego marriage because of religious commitment; to dedicate themselves totally to the worship of God and service to humanity. Those who choose a celibate life their freedom and choice deserve respect.

There are many other reasons, besides religious ones, why some people remain celibate. Some people, for example, cannot marry because of health or physical incapacity. There are also single persons who either fail to find a right partner or who were frustrated by previous partners. Instead of being condemned, these people deserve sympathy and support.

Choice of a Marriage Partner
Marriage is, under normal circumstances, a life long relationship; a personal commitment of a man and a woman to live together for the rest of their lives. It is thus important that a person is bound to a right partner in this important commitment. The choice of a marriage partner at times poses a moral problem. Is it right, for example, for parents to choose a marriage partner for their daughter or son? The dilemma in answering this question is caused by, on the one hand, the experience of parents in marital matters and, on the other, the autonomy of a person who is preparing to undertake marriage.

Different societies have different customs and methods of choosing a marriage partner. In almost all African societies, however, the community is involved in the choice. In some societies, the choice is done by parents, at any time even when the boy or girl is still a baby. If the selection is done when the prospective couple are still very young, they get married when they are old enough to do so and to give their consent. The most common practice is for the parents of a boy to approach the parents of a girl of their choice, around or during the initiation period, and make their intention known. It should be noted, however, that when the choice is made by parents, if either of the couple who intend to marry strongly rejects the proposed partner, marriage does not take place.

There are also cases when the boy is allowed by his parents to make the choice. In that case, if he is accepted by the prospective partner, he seeks the consent of her parents. In all cases, both parties, the prospective couples and their parents, must agree before marriage takes place. It is not acceptable for a young man or woman to marry without the consent of the parents. Parental consent is a *sine qua non* condition, and this is given after consulting the friends, relatives and the family ancestors.

In recent years, Christianity has shifted emphasis from the biological and juridical aspects of marriage to interpersonal, spiritual, and existential aspects. The most stressed feature of marriage is the interpersonal one, which is the living together and the sharing of the life-supporting tasks between the husband and the wife. Marriage is seen as a union resulting from a decision freely and knowingly made by a couple to live together in mutual love and support. The choice of a marriage partner must be made by the two people concerned freely and without either compulsion or hinderance.

The Christian position is that parental consent is sought, but if not granted and two mature people want to commit themselves to one another in marriage, the church accepts them.

In Islam a man or woman has a right to choose a marriage partner. Although ordinarily a man is not permitted to look at a woman with great intent, it is permissible for a Muslim man to look at the woman to whom he intends to propose marriage before actually doing so. This should be done in order to guard against discovering, too late, after marriage, that he does not like her looks or character which could lead to divorce and its consequential problems. However, Islam does not accept mixing freely of men and women or teenage boys and girls. The intending couple must see each other in the presence of the family.

Parents may arrange marriage for their son or daughter, without consulting him or her, but his or her consent is required. If a person is forced to marry, then that marriage is not valid. The father or guardian may not override his or her objections or even ignore his or her wishes. The last word about the marriage partner lies with the parties concerned.

A Baha'i is strongly advised to take utmost care in choosing a spouse. He or she must become thoroughly acquainted with the character of the other because marriage is a life long covenant. The choice, in all situations, is for the two and no one, not even the parents, have a right to interfere with the choice of the two parties involved.

Once the choice has been made, however, the couple must seek and receive the consent of their respective parents. Before a Baha'i marriage can take place, the consent of all living parents is required. This applies always, whether the parents are Baha'is or not, divorced or not. This requirement is necessary because, according to the Baha'i Faith, marriage does not only bind the couple, but also their respective families as well. It is also enforced in order to promote the permanence of marriage. If any of the parents objects to the marriage, it cannot take place.

The marriage contract is so involving that it should be entered into by individuals with mutual love, independent choice and free consent. In marriage, the parties transfer to each other certain rights and accept duties to each other. In addition, marriage imposes so many heavy burdens on an individual that no one else should impose it on him or her. Marriage also presupposes and goes with love and no one can love a person for a son, daughter or friend.

However, those who choose to marry should have reached the age of consent with full knowledge of the nature of marriage with its advantages and demands before they take the serious step to surrender themselves to each other. If marriage is rushed into, it could lead to disastrous consequences. It is important, therefore, that an individual, man or woman, decides, without pressure or hinderance and with full knowledge of what he or she is doing, whether to marry or not, and who he or she shall or shall not marry. This does not mean that parents' advice should not be sought nor should it be ignored. The high rate of separation and divorce these days is partly due to not seeking, or listening to, parents' advice before marriage.

Cohabitation
Cohabitation takes different forms, but basically it is the living together of a man and a woman without, or before public, marriage. Cohabitation may be a temporary arrangement, without the intention of total commitment or living together for life. It may also be done for purposes of finding out whether the two can live together happily as husband and wife; in such cases it is an exploratory arrangement. Cohabitation, however, may be a permanent intentioned arrangement by which a man and woman stay together in total commitment, pending public declaration.

Some people think that there is nothing wrong with cohabitation for any pair who think that they love each other and treat each other with consideration and respect. On the other hand, those who believe in moral absolutes regard cohabitation as wrong.

In African religions marriage is a contract binding a man and a woman and their respective families. The wedding is a public announcement of the decision of a man and a woman that they are ready to unite and form a new family unit. This involves all members, living and dead, of the two families. A decision by a man and a woman, to privately live together as husband and wife is not recognised as marriage.

Christianity does not accept cohabitation and regards it as morally wrong. According to Christianity, marriage is a public testimony of a man and a woman that they are committing themselves to one another and thereby assuming all the duties as well as privileges of marriage. If the couple are Christians, they should seek the blessing and support of the church. Short of this, any arrangement involving sexual intercourse, even with mutual commitment, is regarded either as fornication (1 Cor. 6:18) or as adultery (Ex. 20:14) and, therefore, condemned.

Cohabitation is prohibited in Islam. In Islam, marriage is a life long contract. This is regarded as important to enable an individual to attain the benefit of the repose, affection and company of the marriage partner and for the social goal of the reproduction and upbringing of children in order to perpetuate the human race. This, however, must be lawful marriage contracted publicly and recognised by the society and one's religion. Any other arrangement, made by two individuals privately, is regarded as adultery or fornication.

Sunni Islam even prohibits temporary marriage contracted by two parties to last for a specified period of time (*mut'ah*) because such arrangements do not fulfil the purposes of marriage namely permanence, chastity, reproduction and care for children, love, mercy and a bond between families of the partners involved in the marriage. Shia Islam, however, permits temporary marriages. Prophet Muhammad permitted temporary marriage during the journeys and military campaigns, before the Islamic Regislative process was completed, but later forbade it (Al-Qaradawi Y, 1985: 189).

Cohabitation is not permitted in the Baha'i Faith. In the Baha'i Faith companionate or trial marriage, as it is sometimes called, is immoral and unacceptable. Marriage should be properly conducted, publicly, in the presence of at least two witnesses in order to be recognised. Cohabitation is regarded as another form of fornication.

The essence of marriage is the commitment of a man and a woman which involves loyalty, trust and devotion to each other. Although the witness to this commitment by either the state or by the church is important, it is not the essence of marriage. The ceremony is only a publication to friends, the families, church or the general public what has already taken place. Therefore, to condemn as adulterers a man and woman who love each other and are committed to one another, simply because they have not announced their marriage is questionable and insensitive.

It is true, however, that a marriage which has not been publicly declared is easier to break than that which has been witnessed by the community. The situation becomes worse when the cohabitants or one of them is a student, still working on his or her studies. Whereas cohabitation with commitment may be marriage, it is not prudent to undertake it because there is less security and stability in it; two elements which are important for stable family life and the proper upbringing of children.

Polygamy
Polygamy means marriage to more than one spouse. In a situation where there is one man and two or more women, this is referred to as polygyny. There are also some cases, though rare, where one woman is married to two or more men; a type of marriage known as polyandry.

There is a distinction between simultaneous and successive polygamy. Simultaneous polygamy refers to a situation where a man or woman has more than one spouse at the same time. Successive, also known as serial, polygamy refers to a situation of marriage followed by separation or divorce and remarriage to another partner.

Among other things, marital ethics concerning polygamy centres on issues of fairness, the primary and secondary aims and ends of marriage, and faithfulness. A people's culture and religion play a major role in determining the marital ethic at a given time in a given society.

African religious ethics supports polygamy, commonly in a form of polygyny. Whereas polyandry is rare, polygyny is a common practice in African societies. Both simultaneous and successive polygyny are practised but the most common form is simultaneous polygyny. The man either lives with and supports all his wives and their children in one homestead or he owns several homesteads, one for each wife, and visits them by rotation. In African religious thinking, this is normal and acceptable because polygyny promotes the growth in numbers of the family and of the clan. In some situations, such as when a man dies leaving a young wife, a brother with a wife or wives may be asked by the elders to marry the widow and raise his brother's children.

There are many reasons why traditional societies support polygyny. One of these is that a high value is attached to human life and, therefore, to a big number of children in the family. Polygamy fulfils this by ensuring that many children are born to the family. As Mbiti notes, "He who has many descendants has the strongest possible manifestation of 'immortality', he is 'reborn' in the multitude of his descendants and there are many who 'remember' him after he has died physically; and entered his 'personal immortality'" (Mbiti J, 1969: 142).

Polygyny is also encouraged in order to provide support in the case of a widow who is left without help after the death of her husband. After war, in which many men have died, polygyny helps to cater for the surplus women in society, thus forestalling evils of prostitution, adultery and concubinage.

Polygyny is also used to promote family planning. In most societies, sexual intercourse is forbidden during the period of lactation and polygyny helps the man to satisfy his sexual needs and not to get involved in adulterous affairs. Another reason is that in a polygamous situation, in times of need, there is someone to help. For example, in case of sickness of a wife or when she has given birth, there are other wives to care for the children and the husband. If one wife dies, the other wives take care of her children.

Successive polygyny by which a man sends away his wife, stops supporting her, and takes another wife is also tolerated but discouraged.

It is almost a universal tradition in the major churches that monogamy is obligatory and polygamy is regarded as immoral. It is usually held that whereas polygyny was licit in the Old Testament, this permission was abolished by Christ and monogamy, God's original intention about marriage, was reinstated. This has generally been taken as evident from Scriptures, but the scriptural argument seems to be inconclusive by itself.

In the Old Testament a tendency towards monogamy appears throughout and it was the normal practice and ideal among the Jews of Jesus' time. Polygyny, however, is treated as normal and licit (Ex. 21:10; Lev. 18:18; Dt 21:15-17 etc) Once a king is condemned for taking too many, and especially foreign wives (Dt. 17).

The majority of texts which seem to favour monogamy can be read in a polygamous context as well, if it is accepted that each union is a true marriage and that polygyny does not involve divorce or adultery. The metaphor of Yahweh's love for Israel in marital terms, which churches often use to condemn polygamy, can also be read in a polygamous context. As Israel is a corporate personality, a group of wives are incorporated into the husband's family or clan (Jer. 3:6-10; 31:31-33; Ez. 23: 2-4).

The New Testament's position on polygamy is neither straight forward nor clear. There is no single text which expressly forbids polygamy or decrees monogamy. The Gospel texts which are popularly used to advocate monogamy (Mt. 5:31-2; 19:3-9; Mk 10:2-12; Lk 16:18) deal with divorce and remarriage. In these texts successive polygyny is condemned, but simultaneous polygyny is not dealt with. On the contrary, there is no sign of disapproval of the levirate custom (Mt. 22:23-30), which implies a kind of polygyny. In addition, Paul teaches that converts should remain in the state they were called (1 Cor. 7:12-20). Although the matter is not mentioned, some Jewish converts may have had several wives.

In Timothy and Titus, a minister must be the husband of one wife (1 Tim. 3:2, 12: Tit. 1:6). Although this could mean a second marriage, after the death of the first wife, the texts seem to refer to polygyny. Polygyny is prohibited for church leaders not for other followers. The New Testament comparison of marriage with the church and Christ is not conclusive either for as with Israel, the church is a corporate personality.

Simultaneous polygyny is not condemned in the New Testament, although it existed among the Jews. What is rejected is divorce, polyandry and successive polygyny (Mt.5:27-32; Mk., 10:2-12; Rom. 7:2-3; 1 Cor 7: 2-16; 6:9-18; Eph. 5:22-33). The New Testament is silent about simultaneous polygyny and this could be interpreted as accepting it. Nevertheless, because of Western culture, missionary churches condemn polygyny.

The Islamic view is that Islam is a way of life which is consonant with nature, providing human solutions to the complex situations it confronts, while avoiding extremes (Al-Qaradawi, Y, 1985: 190). This is the case regarding polygamy. According to Islam, a Muslim is permitted to marry more than one woman in order to resolve some very pressing problems facing either the individual or the whole society.

Polygyny in Islam is permitted as a concession, in cases of extreme necessity and in exceptional situations. At the same time, limitations and conditions on it are prescribed. While permitting marrying more than one wife, for example, Islam restricts the number to four, at any given time. It is reported that the case of the Prophet, who himself had nine wives, was exempted from this by Allah for the sake of the propagation of the message of Islam during his life time and because of the needs of the Muslim community after his death (Al-Qaradawi Y, 1985: 191).

Islam puts a condition for a Muslim to marry more than one wife, namely that he must deal equitably with his wives in matters of food, drink, housing, clothing, expenses and in the division of his time between them. As the Quran shows, this seems to be an impossible condition (4:129). The Quran further says that if a person knows that he cannot fulfil this condition to treat his wives equally and justly, he is prohibited by Allah from marrying more than one (4:3) This then seems to suggest that polygyny, though permitted, is discouraged. Polyandry is prohibited because Islam regards it as unnatural.

The Baha'i Faith teaches that the principle of justice must be applied to marriage and since no man can treat several wives equally, a man should have one wife, and a woman one husband. A Baha'i, therefore, is not allowed to take a second wife, but if he already has more than one wife at the time he becomes a Baha'i, he should keep them as his wives because it would be unjust for him to get rid of any of them (Lowell, 1987: 77).

Polygyny in Africa is an institution which was misunderstood by early missionaries and colonialists who wrongly attributed it to African male lust or selfishness. The churches' militant rejection of polygyny seems to be based more on Western culture than on the Scriptures.

Polygamy is a valid form of marriage and, in the past, it ensured the prosperity and growth of the extended family which was necessary at that time and served the interests of both men and women. Polygyny at times was an expression of love. Instead of divorcing a wife who was childless, for example, another one was married. As Shorter observes, simultaneous "Polygamy is the kindest solution in the case of the first wife's infertility. She would prefer to remain a first wife, rather than be divorced and be faced with the impossible task of finding another husband" (Shorter A, 1973: 173). Thus, polygyny was used to prevent divorce which is a greater evil. Simultaneous polygamy, in the form of levirate and widow inheritance, was a way of catering for unsupported women in society for their emotional and other needs. A man who inherited the widow and the children deceased brother performed all the duties of the husband and father. Polygyny also helped to ensure status and support for a woman who could not be first wife, in a society with more women than men and at a time when women had no vocation other than marriage and having children. In societies where women had to do most of the work in the homestead and in the fields, a second wife was a help to the first wife. In addition, in the absence of modern family planning methods, polygyny enabled a wife to have longer time of abstinence from sexual relations during breast-feeding.

This is not to say that polygamy does or did not have problems. Often there are tensions, quarrels and fights between co-wives, but as Shorter observes, "Tension between co-wives is catered for by custom and the attempt is made to minimise them by careful grading of the wives, careful delimiting of their rights and duties, separating their huts and even their homesteads" (Shorter A, 1973:174). This does not mean that partiality on the side of the husband and jealousy among the wives is completely eradicated, but it can be minimised.

Polygamy has some disadvantages, especially for women and children, which include a subordinate position for a wife, the distance of the father from his children and lack of the ideal partnership between a husband and a wife. So as an institution, polygamy has its strengths and weaknesses.

The situation has changed and, although polygyny does not prevent the primary end of marriage in African societies namely procreation of children and their upbringing, monogamy preferred since it ensures the educative influence of the father over his children and the warmth of his company. If we recognise that in marriage mutual love and community of life are as important as procreation, then monogamy is preferable to polygamy. Again in recognition of the full equality of a man and a woman and partnership in a marriage relationship, monogamy is preferred.

Polygyny seems to be irreconcilable with the emancipation of women. Besides, there is no longer need for many children, and sure methods of birth control are readily available. In addition women, even when not married, can comfortably live on their own. So the factors which necessitated having more than one wife are no long as strong as they used to be and as such there is no compelling need for polygyny.

Nevertheless, this does not mean that polygyny, even today, should not be tolerated or even recommended, if conditions dictate. Many people will find polygyny a better alternative to divorce and remarriage. Certainly, simultaneous polygyny seems to be a lesser evil, if it is an evil at all, than concubinage and successive polygyny which are very common in Western societies, the very societies which attack simultaneous polygyny.

Divorce
Marriage is generally regarded as a life long relationship. In many cases, however, this does not happen resulting either in annulment, separation or divorce. Annulment refers to a declaration by a judicial authority that marriage was invalid and, therefore, never existed. Separation, on the other hand, is a decision by authority or by the couple to dissolve community of bed, board or home while the marriage remains in existence. In this section, we are mainly concerned with divorce which is the dissolution of marriage, valid in statutory, customary or church law, so that it ceases to exist. Divorce may come about as a result of a unilateral repudiation of marriage, mutual consent, return of bride gifts, or judgement by a competent court of law.

The normal expectation in African religions is that marriage is a permanent arrangement. Divorce is generally disliked because of its effects on the children and the families involved. It is only accepted as a regrettable last resort. Once the contract of marriage has been executed and rituals performed, it is hard to dissolve it. This is because marriage is not merely a contract between the couple only, but involves many people and families. Similarly, its disruption concerns the relatives and the community.

Whenever marriage problems arise, all those interested parties participate in finding a solution and bringing about reconciliation. It is a great shame and scandal for a man or woman to be responsible for divorce. It is believed that ancestors, too, do not approve of divorce.

However, there are cases where divorce is accepted as a necessary evil. The just reasons for divorce include continuous cruelty by the husband, practising sorcery or witchcraft by the wife or husband, continued unfaithfulness by the wife and desertion of one partner by the other. Sterility and barrenness are not good grounds for divorce. When, for example. The husband is sterile, a brother may 'quietly' perform the sexual duties on his behalf, thus saving the marriage. On the other hand, if the wife is barren, the husband may take her sister or any other woman, but keeps the first wife.

In case of disagreements or when there is a quarrel between a husband and wife, when a man beats his wife or when a wife is mistreated by her co-wives or in-laws, a woman may return to her home for sometime until the husband comes to settle the problem. Temporary separation is common and acceptable but divorce occurs as the last resort when all means to save the marriage have failed.

There is no uniform position taken by all churches on divorce. Nor are the Scriptures clear on this issue. In the Old Testament the Mosaic law does not legislate for divorce, but supposes it, and places certain limitations on it. A writ, for example, must be given so that the divorced woman can marry again, but not to her former husband nor to a priest (Dt. 24:1; 22: 13-19: 22: 28-9). The formula, "She is not my wife and I am not her husband" is given in Hosea (Hos. 2:4). It is not known, however, how frequent divorce was during the Old Testament times.

The New Testament position on divorce is not clear either. At one point Jesus seems to exclude divorce completely (Mt. 19:3-12; Mk. 10:1-9; Lk. 16:18) by appealing to Genesis (Gen. 1:27; 2:24). Paul, too, excludes it, only tolerating separation (1 Cor 7:10-11). In Matthew, however, divorce is allowed on the grounds of unchastity (Mt. 5:32; 19:9). It is generally agreed that Mark and Luke give the original absolute prohibition and Matthew is providing for some unusual situation in the Jewish church. Paul, too, leaves room for divorce when a pagan spouse deserts a convert to Christianity (1 Cor. 7: 12-16).

Churches differ on their position on divorce. The Roman Catholic church maintains the absolute position of Mark and Paul. Eastern churches accept divorce on a wide variety of grounds in which the marriage is "morally dead". Many Protestant churches, too, permit divorce and remarriage during the life time of the partner, if adultery is proved. Some of them, even accept divorce given by civil courts for any reason, as enough.

All churches allow separation without remarriage and usually see adultery as a sufficient reason for it, and all of them stress in their marriage rites the commitment for life, until death, as a Christian demand.

Islam recognises that marriage is a strong bond by means of which Allah joins a man and a woman and stability of marriage is the normal expectation. When there are disputes and disagreements in marriage the couple are asked to tolerate each other and try to find a solution to their problems. Mutual toleration and patience in marriage are strongly recommended.

However, according to the Quran, when disputes and problems become chronic and the atmosphere unbearable the couple should resort to arbiters for a solution (4:35). If the arbiters fail to reconcile the couple, then, as a last resort, they may divorce and Allah will provide for each of them out of His abundance (4:130). Thus, Islam permits divorce, but strongly discourages it. It is said that among the permitted things, divorce is the most hated by Allah.

Other than incompatibility and frequent disputes, divorce may also take place when a husband becomes impotent and cannot perform his marital duties. Another acceptable cause for divorce is the habitual failing to observe religious duties such as saying the mandatory prayers or fasting, by the partner.

In short, divorce without lawful necessity and before exhausting the possibilities of resolving the conflict, is unlawful and prohibited by Islam. A person is not allowed to divorce his or her spouse for selfish reasons such as marrying another wife or husband and to enjoy a variety of sexual partners.

According to the Baha'i Faith, marriage should be life long and divorce is to be avoided, if possible. Couples should not succumb to tests in marriage. Instead tests should help them to grow in virtue. According to the Faith, since given the fact that the purpose of marriage is unity and not separation and because children need the security of both parents, couples should endeavour to remain married throughout life. However, when need be, especially when there is incompatibility and total aversion between a husband and wife, divorce may be permitted. Thus, divorce is permitted but deeply frowned upon (Lowell J, 1987:76).

There are many reasons which lead to divorce including falling out of love, cruelty, sexual incompatibility, economic considerations or family pressure. The most common reason for divorce seems to be adultery, especially when committed by the wife. The other current cause of divorce is the ease with which people get divorce from courts. It should be added that many young couples are not well prepared for marriage. They enter it without full understanding of its importance, dignity or demands and how to cope with them. Traditionally, boys and girls were thoroughly prepared by their parents and the whole family for marriage. This was especially done during the initiation period. Due to changing of social environment and, circumstances been eroded this preparation has ceased and many young men and women enter marriage ill prepared for it. This leads to divorce later in their lives.

Whereas divorce in traditional societies was discouraged and rarely happened because of the intervention of the respective families, these days even one fight at home may result in divorce. The role of the family in stabilising marriage has been seriously undermined.

Divorce is socially undesirable because its effects on children, the partners, and society as a whole are negative. However, it may be, in some cases, a lesser evil, knowing that an unhappy marriage has very many evil consequences, especially on the children, and may result in one partner killing an other. So when marriage has been ruined beyond repair, divorce should not be ruled out.

Bride-gifts exchange

Several terms have been used to describe the exchange of gifts between the family of the bride and that of the groom, either before or after the wedding; a practice which is very common in Africa. These terms include dowry, bride-price, dower, earnest, settlement, indemnity and bride wealth. Without getting involved in the debate about each of them, it seems that none of them adequately describes the practice of exchanging gifts as part of the institution of marriage in Africa. In fact, most of them are misleading. In this book the term 'bride-gifts exchange', is used to avoid the confusion caused by these terms.

Bride-gifts exchange which is practised all over Africa, in varying degrees though, is a complex institution involving families of both the bride and the groom. This practice is used to stabilise marriage and to cement the relationship between the families of the bride and the bridegroom. The couple and their relatives are involved in raising gifts to give and in sharing those which are received. Ancestors, too, are involved in this exchange of gifts and often a sacrifice is offered to them in the process, or one of the animals received is consecrated to them. In some societies, a bride takes to her new home a cow of her own lineage and drinks its milk. The gifts come in a form of cattle, goats, sheep, articles such as hoes or skins, foodstuffs, and more recently, money. In some societies, the families may exchange brides, but this is very rare. There are also instances, when the groom has no relatives or he is poor and contributes labour to his in-laws.

Early missionaries to Africa had a wrong idea about the institution of bride-gifts and condemned it as selling and buying of the bride as much as they condemned other African cultural values and institutions. Missionaries had the tendency to despise and condemn all African ways of life which did not coincide with theirs. Without making serious effort to understand its rationale of the missionaries misconstrued and misconceived bride-gifts exchange and strived to stop it. With the indigenisation various churches which has taken place during the twentieth century, Christianity accepts the exchange of marriage gifts.

In Islam, *ma'hr*, the gift to be given to the bride before marriage by the prospective husband, is a Quranic injunction. The bride has a right to demand a gift in a form of money or property and the prospective husband must give it. This gift becomes hers and she is free to do whatever she wants with it (2:4).

However, the bride is required to be reasonable in her demands (2:236). She should not ask what the prospective husband cannot afford so as to become an obstacle to marriage. Besides, marriage is considered proper even when the gift has not been paid, provided the bride agrees. Gifts to the parents are not compulsory, but if they are asked, and the man can afford to give them, Islam does not prohibit him to give them.

The Baha'i Faith accepts the giving of gifts by the groom's family to the bride's parents. However, a distinction terms of payment is made between a girl who is an urban dweller and one who is a rural dweller. For an urban dweller, the groom pays 19 michcalls of gold while for a rural girl the groom pays 19 michcalls of silver. The equivalent in money, cows or any other form of payment, varies depending on the existing value of gold and silver at the time when the gifts are to be paid. At the moment the payment would be approximately 360 US dollars and 260 Us dollars, respectively. If a young person does not have money to pay, he can give a promissory note to pay when conditions permit.

Early missionaries and colonial authorities misinterpreted bride gifts exchange which they found in most African societies. As a result, they condemned it as bride price, of buying and selling of a woman. This was certainly not the case. Bride-gifts exchange was not a form of payment. The indigenous words for this practice are clearly different from those used in buying and selling. It should also be remembered that it is not only the groom's relatives who give presents, but the bride's relatives as well, even though the mode of determining the amount is different. In many societies, the gifts do not have to be given before the wedding. Among the Swazi, for example, *lobola* is given after the wedding and sometimes many years later. In some societies, the gifts given by the bridegroom to his in-laws is so small that it could not represent the real value of the bride. Among the Banyankore and the Zulu of South Africa, for example, a bridegroom could give only one hoe. This was clearly a symbolic expression of the inner value of the bride not expressed in any other way. Among the Banyankore, on sending off the bride her relatives have to present gifts *emihingiro* to her husband's family to strengthen the bond between the two families and to give the young couple property to start their new home with.

It is not possible to describe and to discuss in detail the practice and value of bride-gifts exchange and the social value of this practice here. It is enough to say that bride-gifts exchange is an important institution which is used to show gratitude on the part of the bridegroom's people to the relatives of the bride for giving them a wife. The practice helps to stabilise marriage and to symbolise the marriage covenant between the two families. The gifts legalise her membership in the new home and the marriage contract. Whereas this practice has both strengths and weaknesses, bride-gifts exchange is morally acceptable and appreciated in most African societies for purposes of legalising and stabilising marriage, legitimising children, propitiating the ancestors of the family and giving cohesion to the extended family (Shorter A, 1973: 171).

The substitution of money for cattle or other symbolic objects such as hoes or goats and the general changes in tradition has rendered bride-gifts exchange much more open to abuse. In some societies the abuse of bride-gifts exchange has become a serious moral problem leading to greed, exploitation of women, delaying or preventing marriages, marital break down and cohabitation without marriage.

Whereas traditionally it was the parents and the families of the groom and of the bride to raise the gifts, nowadays many cannot afford to do so, in which case the task is left to the future husband with or without assistance from friends and relatives. Where the husband raises the gifts himself, the practice gets a new function as a measure of his seriousness and a proof of his own ability. It also ceases to be a cementing factor between the two families or a stabiliser of marriage. Instead it operates against the extended family. In its original form, meaning and practice, bride-gifts exchange served a commendable and useful purpose.

Chapter Eight

FAMILY LIFE

The family, in any given society, occupies a central position in personal and social life because of its traditional roles of regulating procreation and of socialising the new members of society. The family is the first link between an individual and the wider community and a microcosm of society. Besides the procreational and educational functions, the family plays economic, security, health, affectional and recreational roles. Because of these roles, the stability of the family is important for the welfare of society.

As a result of the foreign and modernising influences which have exerted tremendous pressure on African societies, there has been a change in the African family life. As a result, there is a tendency to shift from big to small family units and a variety of family patterns have emerged or are emerging, creating moral problems.

Family patterns

The nature, composition and functions of a family differ from society to society and from time to time. In Western societies, the family as an institution, refers to members of a household which includes a man, his wife and their children. In Africa, a family centres around a man and his wife or wives, his unmarried children, his married sons and their wives and children who are staying with him, his unmarried brothers and sisters and sometimes his elderly mother and even grandparents. The family is the entire group of close relatives.

For many people, however, this type of family has changed and the extended family does not constitute the closest social unit to which one belongs. Kinship bond, deriving from common blood or affinity, is expressed in new forms. The most common emerging form is what is popularly known as "conjugal family" of a husband, wife and their children.

Another form of family life that is emerging is the single parent family. Traditionally, sexual intercourse was limited to marriage and sex outside marriage was regarded as taboo. Urbanisation and Western education have created an environment which changed this ethic. Sex, for young unmarried people, has become a leisure activity for pleasure and sometimes for money. The result is that many girls become pregnant before marriage, and after the first child there is a second and a third or even more. Some of these women fail or refuse to marry. The result is a single parent family of a woman with her children. At times this happens to young men as well. This type of family is related to but different from a one-parent family which is a result of divorce or death of a spouse.

Another trend which is emerging in Africa is for a man or woman to remain single. There are individuals who live by themselves, away from relatives, without close interaction with them. Some women or men remain single because they have failed to get a marriage partner, but others remain so by choice. This seems to be more common among the educated class who favour singlehood in order to avoid inconveniences of marriage and the responsibilities of family life. Although strictly speaking singlehood is not a family pattern, it is a way of life which differs greatly from the traditional family life.

In the African traditional setting, the family is the core of society and the basis of communitarian living to which society attaches high value. An individual experiences life through the family and one is, first of all, a constituent of a particular family which defines who he or she is and who he or she can be.

The family is a complex institution with horizontal and vertical dimensions. The vertical dimension is made up of the dead and those about to be born. The horizontal one consists of the already born living members. A person is positioned at the point where the two lines meet. The family is also a link between the individual and the clan. This is a physical, biological, and social link. Thus, the family is an important unit and everyone has a role to perform in it. A person exercises his or her rights and performs his or her duties in the family according to age and position in relation to other members. Failure to do so is morally wrong.

In the Bible and in Christian ethics, the family occupies an important position. In fact, Christianity is a religion based on the family which became a tribe, a nation and then the chosen people. The family, according to the Christian faith, was instituted by God and the family bond was first made sacred by God himself (Gen. 1-3). The relationship between husband and wife is the core of family life around which mutual responsibility and activity revolve.

In the ideal Christian family, a man leaves his own parental family to cleave to his wife and the two become one flesh (Gen. 1:27; 2:24; 5:21). In this family, the husband is the head (Gen. 3:16), the wife obeys him (Eph. 5:22) the children honour both their parents (ex. 20:12; Deut. 5:16; Eph. 6: 1-6) and parents bring up children in discipline and instruct then in the Christian faith (Eph. 6:4). The structure of the family is permanent (Mk. 10:2-12) and divorce is strongly discouraged (Mt. 19:1-12; 5:27-32). The Christian ideal, too, is a monogamous family of father, mother and children with mutual responsibility (Eph. 5:21-25; Col 3: 18-19). Deviation from this is regarded as wrong.

Islam attaches great importance to family life and regards the family unit as the basis of society. Islam describes the kind of relationship which should exist between a husband and his wife and between parents and children in order to create stable families which will produce harmonious communities.

For the promotion of stable families, Islam advocates marriage and forbids fornication and adultery so that paternity may be realised without doubt or ambiguity. Through marriage, a woman is reserved for one man "thus every child born to her in wedlock will be her husband's child, without any need for recognition or public proclamation of the fact by him or a corresponding claim on the part of the mother" (Al-Qaradawi Y, 1985: 221). The Quran advocates a harmonious relationship between husband and wife in the family (30:21). Harmony, love and compassion in Islam are ideals for founding a happy family.

The Baha'i Faith, too, attaches great importance to the family because the Faith regards the family as a nation in miniature and the nation as a microcosm of humanity. Consequently, according to the Faith, the conditions surrounding family life, embrace the nation and humanity as a whole.

The Baha'i Faith teaches that all members of the family have duties and responsibilities towards one another and to the family as a whole, varying from member to member, according to their natural relationships. The parents have the duty to educate the children and the latter have to obey the parents. The mother has the responsibility of bringing up the children and of creating in her home such conditions as would be conducive to the advancement of the material and spiritual welfare of everyone. The husband has the duty to support the wife in her duties, but his chief responsibility is to provide for and protect the family. Of utmost importance is unity in the family.

Basically, there are two aspects to the family namely a relationship and an institution. The relationship aspect is realised in the institutional one. The changes which are taking place in Africa have affected the family more as an institution than a relationship.

As a relationship, the family refers to the bond between a group of people based on consanguinity or on affinity. Whereas the structure, size and composition of family as an institution in Africa is changing, the bond of family relationship is relatively strong. People still get their emotional, material and social satisfaction, security and support from members of the family. But this, too, is becoming weaker resulting in undesirable practices such as divorce, deserting old people in rural areas, and abandoning babies and street children. The new forms of family life which are emerging are creating new moral problems. Revitalising African family life will go a long way to solve some of these problems.

The change from the traditional extended family to small family units has both advantages and disadvantages. The husband and wife, for example, get closer and more intimate; there is more freedom to share, to understand and to confide in one another instead of confiding in parents. The parental control on the couple is lessened and the wife's role and dignity in the home are enhanced.

However, small units have their own problems. They can, for example, lead to excessive individualism and selfishness and, at times, loneliness. The traditional values of sharing and mutuality are marginalised. This tendency should be controlled in order to preserve mutuality and the family bond.

The status of women in the family

The subordination and exploitation of women has been virtually universal. Consequently, the status of women in the family, and in the society as a whole, is a world wide issue. There is a struggle by women for liberation from male dominated institutions. The situation so far has been for men to rule and women to work. This has far-reaching moral implications.

Most African societies, especially patrilineal ones, are male dominated, in which a woman occupies a subordinate position. A woman is generally regarded as a junior partner who must fear and respect her husband. She is not only supposed to obey her husband, but must serve him without question. A good wife, for example, should not argue with her husband or contradict him on any issue especially in the presence of other people.

A woman is only a home-maker who looks after children, prepares food for the family, keeps the house and surroundings clean and grows food for the home. She is not an equal partner with her husband, but a junior, who under normal circumstances, is expected to rely on her husband on what to do and how to do it, except in the ordinary duties which she carries out daily. Other than routine, a woman does not take serious decisions to make in the home, but relies on the husband's word.

Even outside the home, a woman's human rights are often violated and she is treated as inferior to a man. A woman must show respect to men, whether she knows them or not. During important meetings, a woman does not mix with men unless she is invited and speaks only when permitted to do so. Whatever influence a woman exercises in the family is subject to her husband ultimate approval. Only when a woman has become old and a grandmother, does her status significantly improve. She is then respected and consulted on important matters of the family.

However, there are some religious roles in society which are performed by women as diviners, mediums, rain controllers and medicine experts. These are the channels for women to exert their influence as human beings. Here, more than in any aspect of life, traditional values need to be transformed.

In Christianity, the situation of the woman is not much different. The earlier account of creation has the man created first, and woman from him, named by him, and whose role is to complement him. The woman also yields first to temptation and tempts man (Gen. 2: 18-23: 3:1-7). In Deuteronomy (Deut. 17:

16-17), and in the tenth commandment a woman is grouped with horses and silver, as a man's property. In the latter account of creation, however, man and woman are simultaneously created in the image of God with dominion over the earth and thus fundamentally equal (Gen. 1: 26-28).

In the New Testament, Jesus treated women as equal persons, and he received their ministrations, financial support and preached to them (Lk. 8:3; 10:38-42; 23:56). Notably, in all the gospels, women are the first witnesses of the resurrection and at Pentecost the Spirit came to both men and women. However, Jesus did not radically change their position. No woman, for example, was chosen to be among the twelve disciples, the Lord's Supper was instituted in the presence of men only, and the Apostolic commission was given to men only (Jn. 20:19-23; Mt. 28: 16-20). The status of women is kept low by Paul. While saying that in Christ there is neither male nor female, in practice Paul wants women to observe the subordination to men of the Jewish tradition and of his time (Gal. 3:28; 1 Cor. 14:33-6; 11:3-16; Eph. 5: 24-33; etc).

According to Islam differentiation in sex is neither a credit nor a draw back for the sexes. Islam teaches that what makes one valuable and respectable in the eyes of Allah is neither one's prosperity, position, intelligence, physical strength, sex, beauty or any other biological or social characteristic, but only one's consciousness and awareness of Allah. So spiritually men and women are equal before God. This is stressed by the Scriptures. Concerning the humanity of men and women, the Quran states:

> O mankind! reverence
> Your Guardian-Lord
> Who created you
> From a single Person
> Created, of like nature
> His mate, and from them twain
> Scattered (like seeds)
> Countless men and women.
>   (4:1)

This and other Quranic references (7:189; 42:11; 16:72) show that both men and women were created from the same soul, not a woman being created from the rib of the man.

In terms of rights and responsibilities, the Quran equates a woman with a man (74:38; 3:195; 16:97). The Quran also indicates that marriage is a sharing between the two halves of the society and its bases are love and mercy (30:21).

However, while advocating equality before God of a husband and wife, the Quran teaches that the husband is the protector and maintainer of the wife and that the woman should obey him (4:34). Islam teaches that a good wife should be obedient and submissive in the presence of her husband.

The Baha'i Faith advocates equality of men and women and condemns prejudice against women, which leads men to treat them as inferior beings. According to the Baha'i Faith, women are equal to men before God and they should be treated with equal rights, privileges and opportunities.

The Baha'i Faith teaches that the only relevant difference between people is purity in the sight of God and the righteousness of their life. So whereas men and women have, and may continue to have, different duties in the community, their rights, freedoms and opportunities should be the same.

The struggle for women's liberation from inequalities, exploitation and oppression is at present a universal movement, taking different forms at different stages, and in different societies, religions and cultures. This should be encouraged and supported. The problem, apart from male attitudes, seems to lie in the basic differentiation of male and female biology, psychology and social roles, and how to respect these without discrimination, subordination or disruption of family.

Present trends vary from attempts to do away with distinction between men and women, as totally as possible, in principle and in legislation, so that all functions are open to either, to modifications of the subordinate position of women which can promote equality without disrupting society and within the accepted ideas of the time and place.

The oppression of women should end, but the traditional role of a woman as mother is crucial. The problem here is to reconcile adequate care for her children, especially in infancy, with freedom to engage in professional training and activity. Difficulties that are likely to arise are neglect of children, with problems for them later; neglect of marital obligations, and break up of marriages; conflict between the woman's claim to equality and male expectations of his wife; and financial strains between husband and wife.

It should be recognised that many problems are associated with family traditions and legislation which are based on attitudes of male dominance. Changes in these attitudes can have effects profound on family life. The challenge of today is to initiate these changes wisely without bringing about the disintegration of the African value of family life, a situation that obtains in Europe and North America.

The status of children
Children are developing human beings with physical, psychological and social needs which they, on their own, cannot satisfy. They need physical protection, sustenance, affection, education, and training for adult life, just to mention a

few of their needs. For the realisation of these needs, parental support is indispensable. This does not mean, however, that parents should not respect their children's rights simply because they are dependants.

In African religions, a high value is placed on children and if a marriage is childless, it is regarded as an unsuccessful one. Barrenness and sterility are regarded as a misfortune or even a curse.

Although an African man or woman wants as many offsprings as possible, children are not granted full rights until they are old to have their own homes and families. A child is expected to be obedient, respectful and subservient to his or her parents. At any time, whether he or she likes it or not, a child is expected to serve his or her parents without question, to be told what to do, and not to do what the parents do not accept. A child is totally under the control of the parents.

On the other hand, the parents have a duty to take care of all their children's needs and to protect them from harm. Of most importance is the duty to bring them up properly, according to values and traditions of their society.

Christian ethics places high regard to children as is exhibited in the Bible (Mat. 18:2-6: Lk. 18: 15-17). According to the Old Testament, happy is the family with children (Ps. 127:3, 5). Parents are required to bring up children properly (Prov. 22:6), which in the modern period would include giving them proper school education. Not to bring up children properly is condemned. Although high priority is placed on the education and welfare of children (Deut. 6:7), children are exhorted to honour their parents and to obey them (Ex. 20:12).

The New Testament, too, sees children as a gift from God and children virtues such as innocence, faith and love are required of adults. Thus, in accordance with the above principles and on the basis of the doctrines of divine creation and the dignity of human life, the church condemns abortion, infanticide, child abuse, child labour and any other practice which harms children or deprives them of their rights. The church also advocates proper upbringing of children; physically, intellectually, and spiritually.

Children are highly regarded in Islam and their rights are well protected. The most fundamental right of a child is life. It is for that reason that the Quran prohibits both abortion and infanticide (17:31). A person may not kill what God has designed whatever the reasons, whether economic such as the fear of poverty and lack of provision or for fear of disgrace such as pre-marital pregnancy.

A child has other rights such as sustenance, education and proper care. A Muslim is prohibited to neglect the child's needs or to abuse him or her. Parents are required to treat all their children equally, especially when giving them presents. One should not do more favours to some children and live out others without good reasons. Preferential treatment between one's children is permitted only if a child is handicapped while others are not. All these injunctions are intended to maintain harmony in the family because favouritism arouses enmity and hatred among the children. At the same time, Islam requires children to obey and treat their parents with honour and kindness, and never to insult them.

The Baha'i Faith underlines mutual respect in the family, especially the respect of the rights and prerogatives of each member. This includes the rights of the children.

As the weak and dependant members of the family, children are sometimes neglected and even abused either by their parents or guardians. This poses a moral problem when, for example, children are not adequately fed or properly educated, or when they are assaulted, overworked, or abused in other ways. The parents have the duty to protect, feed, clothe, house and educate their children, while allowing them their deserved freedom and rights. When children's rights are violated or abused this calls for relatives, friends to the family, the community at large, or even the state, to intervene on their behalf.

On the other hand, the children have a duty to obey and respect their parents or guardians and all those who care for them. They are also obliged to participate in family affairs according to their age or ability.

Whereas in some societies the rights and duties of children, in relation to their parents and guardians, end at maturity, in the African context these continue until death. A person is expected to take interest in the affairs of his or her children and to respect his or her parents until death. This is a value which should be maintained as long as individual autonomy and rights are respected.

Family planning

Family planning refers to a decision by spouses, or in some countries by the state, as to how many children are sufficient for a couple and at what intervals they should come. Different people use different methods to plan their families. These include contraception, sterilisation, abstinence from intercourse, intercourse during safe periods only, and withdrawal just before ejaculation. Abortion, too, is used by some women as a method of planning their families. Some of these methods are of moral concern.

Contraception

Contraception refers to any means which allows sexual intercourse but prevents conception. The methods used fall into two broad categories namely mechanical and chemical. The mechanical means may be barrier or intra-uterine devices. Barrier methods such as condoms for males and diaphragms for females prevent the sperm and ovum from meeting. Intra-uterine contraceptive devices such as the loop or coil stop the development of the ovum, after fertilisation. Although these are generally referred to as contraceptives, if the fertilised ovum is seen as genetically determined to become a human being, they are possibly abortificients.

Chemical methods involve inserting substances such as foam tablets, spermicidal jellies, pastes and creams in the vagina to kill the sperms before they reach the ovum. There are also hormonal contraceptive methods by which sex hormones are given to the woman in the form of a pill or injection to prevent ovulation (Namulondo C, 1990:21).

Sterilisation

Sterilisation refers to a procedure by which a man or woman is permanently rendered incapable of reproduction. In the past male sterilisation was accomplished through castration, but this is no longer necessary. These days the procedure is simple, easy, quick and safe, if done carefully and by a knowledgeable doctor. Sterilisation is undertaken for two main reasons namely to prevent pregnancy or for health reasons.

Contraceptive sterilisation may be undertaken by a man by use of vasectomy. This is an operation in which the tubes leading from the testes are tied and cut. After this operation, the man continues to have sexual desires and can perform the sex act as before. His sexual ability is not impaired by the operation. The only difference is that when he ejaculates, there are no sperms in the ejaculate and, therefore, he cannot make a woman pregnant. The sperms which are manufactured in the testes disintegrate when they cannot be used.

A similar operation in a woman is known as tubal ligation. The operation involves tying and cutting fallopian tubes which carry the egg from the ovaries to the uterus. After the operation the woman continues to ovulate and to menstruate. The only difference is that the egg is not able to reach the uterus and so it disintegrates. As in men, this operation does not interfere with a woman's sexual desires and satisfaction. Another method is ovariotomy which entails the removal of both female ovaries, thus stopping the development of the ovum.

These methods of contraception are permanent and cannot be reversed. They are usually used only by those people who are sure that they do not intend to have more children.

Abstinence from sexual intercourse

Abstinence from sexual intercourse may be temporary or permanent. This method may work successfully as a method of family planning, but it may cause more moral problems of adultery, concubinage, neglect of marital duties and other related problems.

Safe periods
There are days when a woman cannot conceive and sex during this time is safe. At a certain time of her menstrual cycle a woman releases an egg from one of her ovaries. It is at this time that she is fertile and can conceive. This (ovulation) takes place roughly between the twelveth and fourteenth day after the first day of her menstrual period. During this period sex may result in pregnancy. Outside these days sex is safe and a couple using this method of family planning abstains from sex during the fertile period.

This, however, seems to be a difficult and risky method to use effectively because many women are irregular in their menstrual cycle and it is difficult to judge when exactly ovulation occurs. In addition, a woman must keep an accurate record of her menses, and it requires the co-operation of both husband and wife.

Coitus interruptus (withdrawal)
Coitus interruptus is a method by which a man withdraws the penis from the vagina before ejaculation. This serves to prevent the sperms from entering the woman, to fertilise the ovum.

For this method to work well, there must be perfect timing and self-discipline. This is extremely important because sperms are good swimmers and can make their way into the vagina even if deposited outside the vulva. This method has an added disadvantage of preventing the full enjoyment of sexual intercourse. As withdrawal is supposed to take place at the time when the urge to go on is very strong and self-control virtually impossible, this method is very unreliable.

As noted earlier on, children are highly valued in traditional religions and a parents try to get as many children as possible. Many children are important for production, security and insurance against old age. Children, however, are most valued for religious reasons namely to ensure immortality of parents, who are believed to be reborn in their children. Children are also wanted for caring for the parents after death. A person without children has no one to pour libation and to attend to him or her, as an ancestor. The more children a person has, the more comfortable he or she will be as an ancestor.

Following from the above, no one tries to regulate birth. However, for the good of the already born baby, spacing is encouraged in order to give the baby enough time to grow, before the mother gets pregnant again. Spacing, using the natural method of breast feeding is acceptable and commonly done. Prolonged breast feeding reduces a woman's fertility and a child is allowed to breast feed up to two years. Polygyny makes this possible as the man can give his breast feeding wife time before getting another child with her. In the meantime, he gets sexual satisfaction from his other wives.

The church is not only concerned with human existence, but also with the quality and dignity of human life. The Christian demand is that all human life should be permitted and enabled to develop to the full dignity and quality of living which befit a human being. Consequently, it advocates responsible parenthood.

Most churches leave the decision, whether to plan the family or not to the couple, but stress right motivation, not to do so for selfish reasons. They also caution against dangers of side effects, advocate seeking medical advice, and oppose indiscriminate distribution of contraceptives. The Roman Catholic church differs fundamentally from most churches on this issue. The Roman Catholic church opposes use of 'artificial' contraceptives as a method of family planning.

According to the Catholic church, every act of intercourse must be open to conception. As such, though advantage may be taken of safe periods, which do not interfere with the act as such, artificial contraception is rejected because it always involves a direct positive action against the possibility of life. However, Roman Catholic ethical thinking is positive. It stresses parental vocation, unity in love and responsible parenthood, excluding materialistic and consumer attitudes towards sex. The church teaches that if there are serious reasons to space out births, which derive from physical or psychological conditions of the husband or wife, or from external conditions, it is licit for the couple to take into account the natural rhythms and regulate births. In other words, the church accepts family planning which respects ethical norms and criteria of the church. The use of natural rhythms is permitted as a means of family planning on the ground that it never involves a direct positive action against the possibility of life.

The position on voluntary sterilisation varies among Christian groups. Protestant Christians generally accept sterilisation as a legitimate method of contraception. Official Roman Catholic teaching, however, condemns contraceptive sterilisation because it is a mutilating act, not required to save one's life or preserve bodily integrity. There are some Catholic theologians, however, who accept contraceptive sterilisation as a morally justifiable act of conscience, if it is chosen for sufficiently serious reasons.

Sterilisation is at times undertaken for therapeutic reasons, to protect the health of a person being sterilised. Many Protestant theologians accept therapeutic sterilisation. In the Catholic church therapeutic sterilisation is permissible only as an unintended, an indirect effect of a procedure whose primary goal is to remove a pathological organ. (Childress J, 1986: 606).

Islam teaches that the preservation of the human race is the primary objective of marriage and such preservation requires continued reproduction. Consequently, Islam encourages Muslims to have many children. However, when a Muslim has valid reasons and recognised necessities such as the preservation of the life of the mother, economic necessities which might lead to doing something prohibited by Islam, the health or the upbringing of the children, he or she is allowed to plan his or her family. While accepting contraception, Islam requires the agreement and co-operation of both partners. But, any method of birth control which restricts or eliminates conception for ever, whether applied to a male or female, is not allowed. Thus, castration, ovariotomy, vasectomy and tubal ligation are forbidden. The only exception is when conception threatens the life of the mother.

In the Baha'i Faith, both the Bab and Baha'u'llah emphasised the need of children in marriage. The Bab, for example, said that to beget children is the highest physical fruit of a person's existence (Hornby H, 1988: 345). Thus, whereas there is no direct or explicit Baha'i teaching on birth control, the general the interpretation of Baha'i teachings is that practices such as birth control should be discarded as constituting a danger to the very foundations of social life.

Marriage is primarily for producing children, to bring other souls into this world to serve God and love Him. Marriage, therefore, has a moral and social purpose which goes beyond the personal needs and interests of the couple. Birth control, therefore, except in exceptional circumstances and cases, is not allowed (Hornby H, 1988: 345). This does not mean that a couple is obliged to have as many children as they can produce. It is up to a couple to decide on how many children they should have, but the method recommended for regulating birth is self-discipline and restraint.

Sterilisation, according to the Baha'i Faith, has far reaching implications than simply limiting the size of the family. It is thus prohibited except in rare cases when it is necessary for medical reasons (Hornby H, 1988: 341).

Family planning is advocated on public level as a method of population control and at individual family level for purposes of regulating births. While recognising the problems of population explosion, there is yet a more fundamental problem. Population growth is associated, among other things, with poverty. There is a remarkable correlation between certain kinds of improvement in socio-economic conditions and a lower birth rate. Thus, the propaganda to reduce birth rates with contraceptives reveals a failure to redress the imbalance between the rich and the poor; individuals and countries, and as a way of maintaining it to the advantage of the rich. Contraceptives are becoming a channel to avoid the task of social and economic betterment for poor countries.

Economic justice, for example, would ease the demographic-induced problem of poverty. It is certainly possible to feed a much greater population, than the world has to day, by better organisation and proper distribution of the world's wealth. World population is a social and economic problem to be solved by social and economic action, over and above the use of contraceptions. This view is supported by the fact that population in the so-called developed nations stopped growing and even started falling long before the wide spread use of contraceptives. Already the attitude in African countries that numerous progeny is culturally and economically an asset is changing. To use contraceptives as a means of curbing population increase in the world can be accepted as a strong argument, but as a short term solution. In the long term, the increase is not certain and could be negated by many other factors such as war, AIDS, catastrophes, and the decline in birth rate due to increased wealth and education.

On an individual level, however, family planning is at times necessary, more especially because of the duty of responsible parenthood. It is important that a couple plans the number of children they can bring up properly with love, care and proper education and the needed space between them. Parents should consider their income, size of their house and other material factors which are necessary for the well-being of the family. They should also think about the physical and emotional health of both husband and wife and the danger of begetting children who are abnormal and might demand a lot of their time and resources at the expense of their health, happiness or at the expense of the other children. These are important factors when one considers the moral duty of responsible parenthood.

Apart from abortion, there does not seem to be any significant moral difference between natural and 'artificial' methods. After all, some of the methods which are usually referred to as 'natural' are unnatural. This is not to say that they should not be used.

Some people argue that natural family planning which requires periodic continence is detrimental to the mutual understanding of the couple. This may be true but a contrary argument is that because it requires the husband and wife to enter into a special relationship with each other and to co-operate and communicate freely before coming to joint decisions, it may strengthen their mutual love and understanding and thus their married life. On social considerations, this method may also be used.

Perhaps the most controversial aspect of family planning is the non-voluntary sterilisation of persons with diminished competence such as "feeble-minded" people. There is also controversy about punitive sterilisation of sex offenders, for women who have already borne "too many children", or as a requirement by some employers that sterilisation is a precondition to employment in potentially hazardous jobs. These are areas that need special attention.

It should be added, however, that there is unease about the indiscriminate way in which contraceptives are, at times, propagated as a means of birth control. Parents are often uncomfortable about these contraceptives when it is realised that this promotes promiscuity. Abortion, as a method of family planning, creates greater concern.

Society needs to uphold the traditional sacredness of sex, the preservation of virginity for both boys and girls and the high value of family life. Thus, family planning should remain for regulating the size of the family, and should not be a licence for free sex as some young men and women make it.

Chapter Nine

CONCLUSION

It has been shown in the previous chapters, that each of the above religions provides its adherents with guidance in moral matters. However, these are mere guides that one may or may not follow. In the end, everyone is morally responsible for his or her actions. People are not machines and so they have to decide personally on what to do, irrespective of what theories, custom, law or even religions prescribe. A person's religion guides him or her on how to behave, but the choice remains his or hers because religious guidance is not infallible.

In African traditional religions, moral authority lies with elders who are the custodians of the norms and values of society which are embedded in custom. But customs are not always a good authority for moral action mainly because they deal with the old and not the current. New issues, problems and situations are not catered for by customs. Customs, more often than not, reflect the values and interests of the dominant class in society. Thus, customs can be unjust and oppressive.

The oppressed groups are compelled to accept and internalise the customs and cultural elements, imposed by the dominant group, as the society values. If this were not the case, it would be difficult to explain customs which subject women to situations in which they are treated as juniors and they accept this treatment as part of their culture. In many African societies, for example, girls are not recognised as equals to boys, and in others they are even deprived of some human rights such as the freedom to choose a marriage partner. Such customs violate some basic human rights. As such they are questionable guides in moral judgement or decision making. Unjust, cruel and oppressive customs need to be examined and rejected and not to be followed. Cultural relativism, too, weakens custom as a moral authority in making moral decisions. For example, it may be regarded as immoral for a Muganda girl to move with bare breasts while it is normal for a Zulu girl to do so. Customs do not usually give adequate reasons for acting in a particular way. They operate on fear, threat and sometimes on mere conformity. Customs, thus, always need to be examined, replaced or augmented to be able to deal with the existential situation. However, customs and tradition should not be discarded lightly. Sometimes, tradition does not evolve without reasons. It is handed down from generation to generation because of its inherent value and because it works. It, therefore, can be a basis for moral reflection, but not necessarily to be followed.

The revealed religions, namely Christianity, Islam and the Baha'i Faith are not infallible either. These religions have Scriptures which are normative, but these are not straightforward or always reliable guides. First of all, Scriptures need interpretation which requires relevant knowledge of texts and contexts and adequate ability to do so. The absence of this often leads to different, and sometimes wrong or misleading, conclusions. In addition, as Muslehuddin explains, although divine laws are eternal and immutable they do not lose sight of the physical world which is subject to change. As a result, they contain broad principles which are open to interpretation in order to accommodate change overtime and to provide for the growing needs of society (Muslehuddin M, 1984:37). This can cause confusion when different interpretations emerge. Secondly, these texts do not agree on all moral positions and this makes it difficult to say that one particular text is absolute. Some texts in the same Scriptures contradict one another even on the same issue, thus causing confusion. A good example is the gospel contradictory position on divorce (Mk. 10: and Mt. 19 : 9-12). Thirdly, Scriptures, for example the Bible, can be used by people to argue opposite sides of an issue. The best example is perhaps the case of South Africa where both the architects of apartheid and liberation theologians used the same bible to support opposing positions.

As to church authority, and indeed authority in other religious traditions, there are similar reservations. First of all, different churches have often taken conflicting stands on moral issues. The use of contraceptives is one such example. Secondly, the very existence of many denominations casts doubt on, and weakens, them as moral authorities. Thirdly, corruption is not only outside the church institutions. In church, as outside it, one finds people who have misused their positions for personal interests. Fourthly, a religious leader is a person and his or her reasoning or judgement may not be better than that of the person acting. If the religious leader is obeyed, this may lead to acting in the absence of a good reason or out of fear. Fifthly, historically, the church has committed errors such as its opposition to some scientific discoveries and its lack of condemnation of evil regimes like the Nazism or colonialism in Africa. Lastly, religious authority is open to the abuse of power as in the Spanish inquisition and in many other cases. The point is that a person is personally responsible for his or her actions and may not follow external guides blindly.

In moral decision-making, there are cases which cause dilemma and in which moral principles or one's religious teaching cannot help him or her to decide. An individual in such a situation needs to consider the uniqueness of the case. There are situations, for example, when an act has two effects, one helpful and the other harmful, or one good and the other evil. In situations when one's actions have two contradictory results, one may apply *the principle of double effect*. According to this principle it is morally right to perform an action which is itself good or at least neutral, though such action may have two effects one of which is good and the other bad, provided that the action itself is not morally evil; the good effect is primary, or immediate, and the bad effect is secondary; the intention is good, the evil effect is not intended; and there is a proportionately grave reason to do so and to allow evil to occur (Childress J, 1986:162).

This is what happens when a doctor removes a cancerous uterus of a pregnant woman which leads to the death of the foetus. If the doctor does not remove the uterus, the cancer will spread and bring death to both mother and child. In this case there is a proportionately grave reason to perform the operation to save the mother, although the process kills the foetus. This principle is similar to, but slightly different from *the principle of the lesser evil.*

In a situation when a person is confronted with two evil alternatives, he or she is required to choose the lesser one. If, for example, a driver of a bus is confronted with a situation where he or she either will hit a pedestrian or hit an on coming vehicle. It is morally right to hit the pedestrian, if that is the only thing that can be done, the alternative being a head-on collision that will result in the death of many people, which is a greater evil.

One may at times have to follow the *principle of totality.* According to the principle of totality the good of a part may legitimately be sacrificed for the good of the whole. An abscessed tooth, gangrene, or ectopic pregnancy, for example, may call for the application of this principle. Even a healthy part may be sacrificed for the good of the whole. When child bearing, for example, proves a threat to the life of a mother, sterilisation may be done as a method of contraception. This principle is not only applied to organisms, such as human beings, it may, by analogy, be applied to non organic wholes such as the army, the family, or the state. Soldiers dying for the safety of their country or a father undertaking a dangerous job for the sake of his family, if he has no alternative, can be morally justifiable. This principle, however, should not be confused with the view that the end justifies the means. It applies only when the whole's existence is threatened by its part or when a part can save the whole, when the whole is in danger.

At times a person has to do something hateful as a necessary evil. Compromise with evil is not a new thing. Jesus in Matthew points out that Moses had permitted the dissolution of marriage only because of the hardness of people's hearts (Mt. 19:8-9). Islam, too, faces the same problem. It is said in Islam, for example, that divorce is the most hateful of permitted things, in the sight of God. It is permitted as a necessary evil.

In moral decision-making, a person needs to know her or his rights and obligations, the consequences of her or his actions, and in complex situations he or she should seek the guidance of his or her religion or of other moral guides. Good intentions to act well may be misdirected because of ignorance and an honest and sincere person can make honest mistakes. In order to arrive at a correct and right moral decision, one needs to inform himself or herself so that his or her reason or conscience, the ultimate guides a person has, may lead him or her to a correct course of action.

An important question in ethics is: when is a person to be held morally responsible for his or her actions? A person is not morally responsible if he or she lacks the capacity to distinguish between right and wrong or good and bad. A person who cannot make rational value judgements is considered amoral. A person who lacks the capacity to distinguish between right and wrong, either because he or she has not developed it, as in very young or autistic children and the severely retarded, or because he or she has lost it, as in the seriously mentally ill and the senile, cannot be held morally blameworthy.

A fully moral act requires full knowledge and free choice. Whatever diminishes either knowledge or freedom diminishes or destroys free choice and therefore moral responsibility. Ignorance, for example, does that. For ignorance to destroy responsibility, however, it must be total and involuntary in itself. Affected ignorance, when one deliberately avoids knowing whether an act is right or wrong, in order to commit it easily, increases blameworthiness. A person who refuses to inform oneself on some act he or she is about to do is still responsible for it. This is *culpable ignorance*.

The nature of the act is also a major consideration. Some actions are non-moral, meaning that they are morally neutral; neither right or wrong. A person is free to perform such actions. It is morally neutral, for example, for a person to wear a blue shirt instead of a white one. However, human actions which may be non-moral in one set of circumstances, society, religion or place can be moral issues in different circumstances, societies, religions or places. Polygamy, which is a non-moral issue in African traditional religions, for example, is a moral one in a Christian society.

A person is, therefore, morally responsible when he or she acts wilfully, freely and with full knowledge of what he or she is doing and violates a moral rule or neglects to do his or her duty. A person who does something by accident or coercion is not morally responsible.

The morality or immorality of an act does not only depend on the rules governing that act alone. It also depends on the motive for doing it, circumstances in which it is done and its consequences.

As it has been shown in this book, different religions have ways of conduct which are regarded as right and proper for their adherents. All the four have moral rules which their adherents require to keep. They prescribe what is right or wrong conduct, who is a good or bad person and what is a good or bad life. Morality is regarded as one way adherents of a religion use to please the God they worship, to live in harmony within the community and to enjoy blessings from the sacred world.

An aspect of religious ethics which is common to all the four religions discussed in this book is authoritarianism. Each religion has its moral rules which it regards as an infallible guide to proper behaviour for its adherents. These rules are regarded as God's or ancestors' commands which are beyond questioning. Everyone is expected to obey them with or without understanding or agreeing with them. Whoever does not follow them is regarded as immoral and, therefore, deserving punishment from above or from the religious community itself. Sin and immorality are equated.

The point of departure between African religious ethics and the ethics of the other three religions is that whereas the three religions emphasise individuality and individual responsibility, the African ethic advocates corporate existence and mutual responsibility; to be is to belong. Without necessarily undermining individual autonomy, this book advocates a return, where possible, to the African world view. It is this world view which has potential for mutuality, community and unity of humanity.

Not all forms of morality, however, have a religious connection. At times, religion and morality do not require or prohibit the same conduct. The two may even demand conflicting ways of behaviour, especially in a society with a religion which originates from outside. This was, for example, the case when Christianity came to Africa and put demands which conflicted with traditional African ethical values. So whereas religious and moral requirements may overlap, this may not always be the case. Essentially, religion is about what one's God, gods or ancestors demand or desire while morality is about what is beneficial or harmful to human beings or their environment.

In morality, certain forms of behaviour are recommended or prohibited not because religion does not permit them, but because society does not accept them (Tremmel W, 1984:232). As it has been shown, morality does not necessarily depend on religion for it can depend on reason, natural law or other secular guides.

Though religion and morality are not always the same, they are often related and influence each other and even overlap in many ways in a given society. When the two are similar, moral values receive divine sanction and turn into a religious ethic. Whatever guide a person follows, a person is ultimately morally responsible for his or her actions.

REFERENCES

Abdu'l Baha' (1909), *Tablets of Abdu'l Baha'* Vol. 1, Chicago: Baha'i Publishing Trust

Abdu'l Bah' (1981), *Some Answered Questions*, Wilmette, Baha'i Publishing Trust, 1981

al-Qaradawi Y, (1985) *The Lawful and the Prohibited In Islam*, Indianapolis, American Trust Publications

Armstrong K, (1988), *Holy War*, London: Macmillan

Baha'u'llah (1976), *Gleanings from Writings of Baha'u'llah*, Illinois Baha'i Publishing Trust

Crawford R, (1991) *Can We Ever Kill*, London, Harper Collins, Childress J, (ed) (1986), *The Westminister Dictionary of Ethics* Philadelphia The Westminster Press

Contact Magazine, No. 144 May 1990

Cruden A (ed) (1980), *Cruden's Complete Concordance*, Grand Rapids: Zondervan Publishing House

Curran C.E, (1992), *Moral Theology*, Indiana: University of Notre Dame

Cutter R, (1969), *Updating Life and Death*, Boston: Bacon Press

Daughters of St. Paul: (1984, *Pro-life Catechism*, Bostond, Daughters of St Paul

Dewey J, (1936), *Ethics*, New York:;

Fathea'zam H, (1980), *The New Garden*, New Delhi: Baha'i Publishing Trust

Fletcher J, (1960), *Moral and Medicine*, Boston: Beacon Press

Frankena W, (1973), *Ethics*, Englewood Cliffs: Prentice-Hall

Frohock F, (1983), *Abortion*, London: Greenwood

Frommer M, (1983), *Ethical Issues In Sexuality and Reproduction*, Missouri: Cosby Co.

Gallagher J, (1985), *The Basis For Christian Ethics*, New York: Paulist Press

Haralambos M, (1985) *Sociology: Themes and Perspectives*, London: Bell & Hyman

Haselbarth H, (1976), *Christian Ethics in the African Context* Ibadan Daystar Press

Hornby H, 1988), *Lights of Guidance*, New Delhi: Baha'i Publishing Trust

Ikenga-Metuh A, (1987), *Comparative Studies of African Traditional Religions*, Onitsha: IMICO

Kenyatta J, (1938) *Facing Mount Kenya*, London: Secker and Warburg

Kasenene P, (1990) *Religion in Swaziland*, Braamfontein: Skotaville Publishers
Komonchak J, ed. (1988) *The New Dictionary of Theology*, Dublin Gill and Macmillan
Lowell J, (1987) *The Eternal Covenant*, Johannesburg: NSA
Maimela S, "Seeking to be Christian in Patriarchal Society", in *Voices from the Third Word*, Vol. XIX No. I
Mappes T, (1982), *Social Ethics*, New York: MacGraw-Hill
Mbiti J, (1969), *African Traditional Religions and Philosophy*, Nairobi: Heinneman
Mitchell B, (1980), *Morality: Religious and Secular*, Oxford, Clarendon Press
Mosala I (1988), "The Implications of the Text of Esther for African Women's Struggle for Liberation" in *Journal of Black Theology*, Vol. 2
Muslehuddin M,(1984), *Morality: Its Concept and Role in Islamic Order*, Lahore: Islamic Publications
Namulondo C, (1990), *About Family Life*, Nairobi: St.Paul Publications
Narveson J, (1983) *Moral Issues*, Toronto: OUP
Pomedli M, "Cultural diversity enriching Christian religious experience" in *Studies in Religion*, Vol. 20 No 1
Pobee J, (1979) *Toward An African Theology*, Nashville: Abingon
Ramsey P, (1978), *Ethics at the Edges of Life*, New Heaven: Yale University Press
Ratanakul P, (1986) *Bioethics*, Bangkok, Mahidol University Press Reich W, (ed) (1978) *Encyclopedia of Bio-ethics*, New York: Macmillan
Searle C, (1984), *Aspects of Community Health*, Cape Town: King Edward the Seventh Trust
Shorter A 1973) *African Culture and the Christian Church*, London: Geoffrey Chapman
Smith H, (1988), *Essays on Ultimate Questions*, Aldershot: Avebury Press
Taylor P, (1975), *Principles of Ethics*, Encino: Dickenson Publishing Co.
Tempels P, (1969), *Bantu Philosophy*, Paris: Presence Africaine
Thielicke H, (1996), *The Ethics of Sex*, Cambridge: James Clarke
Tremmel W, (1984), *Religion: What Is It?*, Chicago: Rinehart and Winston
UNO(1949) *Universal Declaration of Human Rights*
Verstraelen H, (ed) (1993) *Rewriting the Bible*, Gweru: Mambo Press
Wogaman J, (1976), *A Christian Method of Moral Judgement*, London: SCM Press

INDEX

Abahima 68

Abortion 12, 16, 20, 21, 49-56 65, 76, 99, 100, 105, 106, 112
Abstinence 86, 100, 101
Adultery 12, 63, 64, 66-72, 74, 75, 82-84, 88, 89, 95, 102
Africa 4, 8, 10-12, 22-26, 30, 32, 34, 36, 39, 45, 47, 49, 55, 57, 60, 61, 71, 78, 86, 99, 101, 102, 104, 106, 113
African Religions 10, 24, 30, 31, 33, 38, 42, 52, 63, 65, 67, 70, 72, 75, 77, 81, 87, 99
Alcohol Hepatitis 37
Alcoholism 12, 32, 36,37, 38, 39
Allah 29, 32, 39, 42, 46, 58, 64,78, 85, 88, 89, 97
Anglican 39
Annulment 87
Anti-abortionists 50
Arab 25
Assemblies of God 39
Asthma 32

Baha, Abdul 26, 29, 46, 48, 60
Baha'i Faith 4, 6, 10, 24, 26, 29, 32, 34, 36, 39, 42, 46, 48, 54, 59, 60, 65, 66, 69, 71-75, 78, 81, 82, 85, 89, 91, 95, 98, 100, 104, 107
Baha'u'llah 29, 104, 112
Bakiga 63
Banyankore 8, 35, 63, 91
Batoro 35, 77
Beriberi 37
Bio-ethics 14, 113
Bride price 91
Buddhism 77

Caffeine 34
Calvin, John 21
Celibacy 12, 77, 78, 79
Children 6, 9, 10, 12, 20, 21, 35, 36, 40, 43, 47, 49, 52, 54, 55, 59, 62, 64-66, 70, 71, 77, 79, 82, 84, 86- 89, 91, 93-96, 98 102, 104, 105, 110

Christianity 4, 10, 23-25, 32, 45, 58, 64, 66, 68, 70, 80, 82, 88, 90, 94, 96, 107, 111
Cirrhosis 37
Cocaine 33, 34
Coffee 34, 35
Cohabitation 81, 82, 92
Coitus interruptus 72, 102
Conscience 15-19, 28, 48, 103, 110
Contraception 100, 101, 103, 104, 109
Contraceptives 21, 67, 101, 1-106, 108
Crawford 43, 112
Culpable homicide 45
Culture 11, 14, 25, 26, 40, 83, 85, 107, 113

Dagga 34
Deontological theories 20
Divorce 12, 38, 50, 68, 80, 81, 83-89, 93-95, 108, 109
Domestic Violence 59
Dowry 90
Drug abuse 12, 32–44,

Egypt 25, 26
Ethics 3, 4, 6, 10-12, 14, 15, 19-27, 30, 53, 62, 64, 66, 77, 83, 94, 99, 110-113
Ethiopia 25
Euthanasia 12, 16, 19, 56, 57, 58, 59

Family patterns 12, 93
Family planning 12, 84, 86, 100-106
Farrah 29, 72
Fornication 9, 12, 64, 65, 66, 69, 74, 75, 82, 95

Gastritis 37
Gigolos 70
Gommorah 72

Hadith 29, 72
Hahish 34
Haram 29, 72
Hinduism 77
Holy Spirit 17, 33, 38
Homosexuality 12, 16, 21, 62, 64, 71-73
Hypomania 33

108

Ijma 29, 72
Incest 64
Industry 14
Intuition 15, 16, 17, 19
Islam 4, 10, 24, 25, 28, 29, 32-35, 39, 42, 46, 48, 54, 58, 60, 64, 65, 66, 69, 71, 72, 74, 75, 78, 80, 82, 85, 88-90, 94, 95, 97-100, 104, 107, 109, 112
Islamic ethics 25

Jesus 28, 38, 48, 68, 78, 88, 97, 109

Kitab Aqdas 75

laryngitis 36
lesbianism 62
lung cancer 36

Makruh 29, 35, 72
Marijuana 33, 34
Marriage 3, 10, 11, 12, 16, 20, 25, 26, 38, 49, 62-69, 71, 74, 75, 77-95, 97, 99, 104, 107, 109
Masai 68
Masturbation 12, 62, 63, 66, 73, 74
Mbiti 26, 35, 68, 75, 77, 83, 113
Medicine 14, 31, 34, 37, 39, 96, 112
Meta-ethics 15
Methodist 39
Mohammed, Prophet 25
Monogamy 84, 86
Morals 12, 14, 24, 27, 37, 69, 72
Mormons 34
Mubah 29, 72
Muganda 107
Muslehuddin 108, 113
Muslims 23, 28, 29, 32, 65, 74, 104

Narcotics 34
Natural Law Theory 20, 21, 62
Nazarene 39
Nazarites 38
New Testament 33, 38, 53, 68, 70, 72, 85, 88, 97, 99
Nicotine 34
Normative ethics 15
North Africa 25
Nyakyusa 63

Old Testament 28, 38, 53, 68, 70, 72, 84, 88, 99
Opium 33, 34
Orthodox churches 78

Pancreatitis 37
Pellagra 37
Penal laws 34
Philosophy 14, 15, 27, 113
Pneumonia 36
Polyandry 83, 85
Polygamy 12, 25, 77, 83, 84-86, 110
Polygyny 83, 84, 85, 86, 103
Prostitution 12, 70, 71, 83
Protestant Churches 28, 54, 88

Qiyas 29, 72
Quran 28, 29, 39, 42, 46, 48, 60, 69, 72, 74, 85, 88, 95, 97, 99

Racial intermarriage 16
Rape 40, 54, 55, 63, 64, 70, 71, 74, 75, 76
Roman Catholic 21, 28, 39, 77, 78, 88, 103
Roman Catholic Church 21, 28, 78, 88, 103

Safe periods 100, 102, 103
Schizophrenia 33
Self defence 48
Separation 38, 50, 81, 83, 87, 88, 89
Seventh Day Adventist 35, 39
Seventh Day Adventist Church 35
Sex 3, 9, 12, 21, 25, 26, 40, 60, 62-72, 74-76, 78, 93, 97, 101-103, 105, 106, 113
Sexism 12, 74
Sexual intercourse 63-69, 75, 76, 82, 84, 93, 100-102
Sharia 29
Shia Islam 82
Situation ethics 21, 22
Smoking 12, 35, 36
Sodom 72
South Africa 91, 108
Sterilisation 100, 101, 103, 104, 105, 109
Sudan 25

Suicide 12, 19, 32, 33, 41-44, 56
Sunnah 29, 72
Sunni Islam 82
Swazi 26, 65, 69, 77, 91

Tanzania 63
Tea 34
Teleological theories 19
Ten Commandments 20
Tranquillisers 33

Uganda 4, 8, 26, 35, 40, 68, 72
Universal Declaration of Human Rights 31, 113

Venereal Diseases 66, 69, 76

Wedding 38, 81, 90, 91
West Africa 25
World Health Organisation 32

Zina 72, 75
Zulu 91, 107

www.ingramcontent.com/pod-product-compliance
Lightning Source LLC
Chambersburg PA
CBHW070946230426
43666CB00011B/2578